# Learning Flask Framework

Build dynamic, data-driven websites and modern web applications with Flask

**Matt Copperwaite**

**Charles Leifer**

[PACKT] open source*

PUBLISHING    community experience distilled

BIRMINGHAM - MUMBAI

# Learning Flask Framework

First published: November 2015

Production reference: 1241115

Published by Packt Publishing Ltd.
Livery Place
35 Livery Street
Birmingham B3 2PB, UK.

ISBN 978-1-78398-336-0

www.packtpub.com

# Credits

**Authors**

Matt Copperwaite

Charles Leifer

**Reviewers**

Abhishek Gahlot

Burhan Khalid

**Commissioning Editor**

Ashwin Nair

**Acquisition Editor**

Subho Gupta

**Content Development Editor**

Mamata Walkar

**Technical Editors**

Siddhesh Ghadi

Siddhesh Patil

**Copy Editor**

Sonia Mathur

**Project Coordinator**

Shipra Chawhan

**Proofreaders**

Stephen Copestake

Safis Editing

**Indexer**

Mariammal Chettiyar

**Production Coordinator**

Conidon Miranda

**Cover Work**

Conidon Miranda

# About the Authors

**Matt Copperwaite** graduated from the University of Plymouth in 2008 with a bachelor of science (Hons) degree in computer systems and networks. Since then, he has worked in various private and public sectors in the UK. Matt is currently working as a Python software developer and DevOps engineer for the UK Government, focusing mainly on Django. However, his first love is Flask, with which he has built several products under the General Public License (GPL).

Matt is also a trustee of South London Makerspace, a hackerspace community in South London; a cohost of The Dick Turpin Road Show, a podcast for free and open source software; and LUG Master of Greater London Linux User Group.

He has also been the technical reviewer of the *Flask Framework Cookbook*.

> I would like to thank my new wife Marie who has been so patient throughout the production of this book.

**Charles Leifer** is a professional software engineer with 6 years of experience using Python. He is the author of several popular open source libraries, including Peewee ORM and Huey, a multithreaded task queue. He is also the cocreator of `https://readthedocs.org`, a free documentation hosting platform.

Charles developed a passion for Python while working at the Journal World. His colleagues there patiently answered his endless questions and taught him everything about the Web, Linux, open source, and how to write clean Python.

Charles maintains an active programming blog at `http://charlesleifer.com`.

> I would like to thank my wife, Leslie, and my parents, Anne and John, for their encouragement and support.

# About the Reviewers

**Abhishek Gahlot** is a Computer Engineer and holds a Bachelors degree in Computer Science. He loves programming in Python and Go.

He created two Web Applications Cloudtub (`cloudtub.com`) and Dynofy (`dynofy.com`). Dynofy uses the Flask framework for Web and REST API. Abhishek is very passionate about Algorithms, Artificial Intelligence and Parallel Programming.

He occasionally writes articles related to Web Engineering at `blog.abhishek.it`. Abhishek can be reached at `me@abhishek.it`.

**Burhan Khalid** has always been tinkering with technology from his early days of XT to writing JCL on the ISPF editor, C and C++, Java, Pascal, and COBOL, to his latest favorite, Python. As a lover of technology, he is most comfortable experimenting with the next big technology stack.

By day, he works at a multinational bank in the alternative channels unit, where he gets to hack, develop, and test applications that help execute transactions across all sectors of electronic devices and channels. In addition to his work, he also contributes to open source projects. Burhan has also released a few toolkits for transaction processing.

He is an avid volunteer and has mentored Sirdab Lab (a start-up accelerator). Burhan is a frequent speaker at the local Google Developer Groups, a presenter and volunteer at StartupQ8, a start-up community. He is also actively involved with StackOverflow.

In his free time, you can find him splitting time nurturing his other passions — flight, by scheduling time in flight simulators, and photography, by uploading images to his Flickr feed.

I would like to thank my mother and father for always encouraging me; my wife for putting up with my long days at the keyboard and my ever - growing gadget collection; and my friends and colleagues for providing me with new challenges to sharpen my skills.

Special thanks to **Lalith Polepeddi** for contributing to the book at a stage where we needed it the most.

# www.PacktPub.com

## Support files, eBooks, discount offers, and more

For support files and downloads related to your book, please visit www.PacktPub.com.

Did you know that Packt offers eBook versions of every book published, with PDF and ePub files available? You can upgrade to the eBook version at www.PacktPub.com and as a print book customer, you are entitled to a discount on the eBook copy. Get in touch with us at service@packtpub.com for more details.

At www.PacktPub.com, you can also read a collection of free technical articles, sign up for a range of free newsletters and receive exclusive discounts and offers on Packt books and eBooks.

https://www2.packtpub.com/books/subscription/packtlib

Do you need instant solutions to your IT questions? PacktLib is Packt's online digital book library. Here, you can search, access, and read Packt's entire library of books.

## Why subscribe?

- Fully searchable across every book published by Packt
- Copy and paste, print, and bookmark content
- On demand and accessible via a web browser

## Free access for Packt account holders

If you have an account with Packt at www.PacktPub.com, you can use this to access PacktLib today and view 9 entirely free books. Simply use your login credentials for immediate access.

# Table of Contents

# Preface

Welcome to Learning Flask, the book that will teach you the necessary skills to build web applications with Flask, a lightweight Python web framework. This book takes an example-driven approach that is designed to get you started quickly. The practical examples are balanced with just the right amount of background information to ensure that you understand not only the how, but also the why of Flask development.

Flask was originally released by Armin Ronacher as part of an elaborate April Fool's Day prank in 2010. The project touted itself as, "The next generation python micro web-framework," and lampooned features made popular by similar microframeworks. Although Flask was intended as a prank, the authors were caught by surprise when many people expressed serious interest in the project.

Flask is a microframework that is built on top of two excellent libraries: the Jinja2 templating engine, and the Werkzeug WSGI toolkit. Despite being a relative new-comer compared to other frameworks, such as Django, and Pylons, Flask has garnered a large and loyal following. Flask provides powerful tools for common web development tasks and encourages a bring-your-own-library approach for everything else, allowing programmers the flexibility to pick and choose the best components for their application. Every Flask app is different, and as the project's documentation states, "Flask is Fun".

The Flask microframework represents a departure in terms of design and API from most other popular Python web frameworks, which has led many developers that are new to Flask to ask, "What is the right way to build an app?" Flask does not offer any strong opinions on how we, the developers, should build our app. Instead, it provides opinions on what you need to build an app. Flask can be thought of as a collection of objects and functions to deal with common web tasks, such as routing URLs to code, processing request data, and rendering templates. While the level of flexibility that Flask provides is liberating, it can also lead to confusion and poor designs.

The purpose of this book is to help you see this flexibility as opportunity. Over the course of this book, we will be building and progressively enhancing a Flask-powered blogging site. New concepts will be introduced through the addition of new features to the site. By the end of the book, we will have created a fully-featured website, and you will have a strong working knowledge of Flask and the ecosystem of its commonly-used extensions and libraries.

# What this book covers

*Chapter 1, Creating Your First Flask Application*, begins with the bold declaration, "Flask is fun", which is one of the first things that you see when you view the official Flask documentation, and in this chapter, you will get to grips with why so many Python developers agree.

*Chapter 2, Relational Databases with SQLAlchemy*, says that relational databases are the bedrock upon which almost all modern web applications are built. We will use SQLAlchemy, a powerful object-relational mapper that allows us to abstract away the complexities of multiple database engines. In this chapter, you will learn about how the data model that you choose early on will affect almost every facet of the code that follows.

*Chapter 3, Templates and Views*, covers two of the most recognizable components of the framework: the Jinja2 template language, and the URL routing framework. We will fully immerse ourselves in Flask and see our app finally start to take shape. As we progress through the chapter, our app will start looking like a proper website.

*Chapter 4, Forms and Validation*, shows you how to use forms to modify content on your blog directly through the site handled by the popular WTForms library. This is a fun chapter because we will add all sorts of new ways to interact with our site. We will create forms to work with our data models and learn how to receive and validate user data.

*Chapter 5, Authenticating Users*, explains how you can add user authentication to your site. Being able to distinguish one user from another allows us to develop an entirely new class of features. For instance, we will see how to restrict access to the create, edit, and delete views, preventing anonymous users from tampering with site content. We can also display a user's draft posts to them but hide them from everyone else.

*Chapter 6, Building an Administrative Dashboard*, shows you how you can build an administrative dashboard for your site, using the excellent Flask-Admin. Our admin dashboard will give certain selected users the ability to manage all the content across the entire site. In essence, the admin site will be a graphical frontend for the database, supporting operations to create, edit, and delete rows in our application's tables.

*Chapter 7, AJAX and RESTful APIs*, uses Flask-Restless to create a RESTful API for the blogging app. A RESTful API is a powerful way of accessing your app programmatically by providing highly-structured data to represent it. Flask-Restless works very well with our SQLAlchemy models, and it also handles complex tasks, such as serialization, and result filtering.

*Chapter 8, Testing Flask Apps*, covers how you can write unit tests covering all parts of the blogging app. We will utilize Flask's test client to simulate "live" requests. We will also see how the Mock library can simplify testing complex interactions, such as calling third-party services, such as databases.

*Chapter 9, Excellent Extensions*, teaches you how to enhance your Flask installation with popular third-party extensions. We used extensions throughout the book, but we can now explore the added extra security or functionality with very little effort and can polish off your app nicely.

*Chapter 10, Deploying Your Application*, teaches you how to deploy your Flask applications securely and in an automated, repeatable manner. We will look at how to configure the commonly-used WSGI capable servers, such as Apache and Nginx, as well as the Python web server Gunicorn, to give you plenty of options. Then, we will see how to secure part or the entire site using SSL before finally wrapping up our application in a configuration management tool to automate our deployment.

# What you need for this book

While Python is at home on most operating systems, and we have tried to keep an operating system-agnostic approach within the book, it is advisable to use a computer running a Linux distribution or OS X when working with this book, as Python is already installed and running. The Linux distribution can be either installed on the machine or within a virtual machine. Almost any Linux distribution will do, and any recent version of Ubuntu will be fine.

# Who this book is for

This book is for anyone who wants to develop their knowledge of Python into something that can be used on the Web. Flask follows Python design principles, and it can be easily understood by anyone who knows Python and even by those who do not.

# Conventions

In this book, you will find a number of text styles that distinguish between different kinds of information. Here are some examples of these styles and an explanation of their meaning.

Code words in text, database table names, folder names, filenames, file extensions, pathnames, dummy URLs, user input, and Twitter handles are shown as follows: "We can include other contexts through the use of the `include` directive."

A block of code is set as follows:

```
from app import api
from models import Comment

api.create_api(Comment, methods=['GET', 'POST'])
```

When we wish to draw your attention to a particular part of a code block, the relevant lines or items are set in bold:

```
{% block content %}
  {{ entry.body }}

  <h4 id="comment-form">Submit a comment</h4>
  {% include "entries/includes/comment_form.html" %}
{% endblock %}
```

Any command-line input or output is written as follows:

```
(blog) $ python manage.py db upgrade
INFO   [alembic.migration] Context impl SQLiteImpl.
INFO   [alembic.migration] Will assume non-transactional DDL.
INFO   [alembic.migration] Running upgrade 594ebac9ef0c ->
490b6bc5f73c, empty message
```

**New terms** and **important words** are shown in bold. Words that you see on the screen, for example, in menus or dialog boxes, appear in the text like this: "You should see the message **Hello, Flask** displayed on a blank white page."

[ *(icon)* Warnings or important notes appear in a box like this. ]

[ *(icon)* Tips and tricks appear like this. ]

# Reader feedback

Feedback from our readers is always welcome. Let us know what you think about this book—what you liked or disliked. Reader feedback is important for us as it helps us develop titles that you will really get the most out of.

To send us general feedback, simply e-mail feedback@packtpub.com, and mention the book's title in the subject of your message.

If there is a topic that you have expertise in and you are interested in either writing or contributing to a book, see our author guide at www.packtpub.com/authors.

# Customer support

Now that you are the proud owner of a Packt book, we have a number of things to help you to get the most from your purchase.

## Downloading the example code

You can download the example code files from your account at http://www.packtpub.com for all the Packt Publishing books you have purchased. If you purchased this book elsewhere, you can visit http://www.packtpub.com/support and register to have the files e-mailed directly to you.

# Errata

Although we have taken every care to ensure the accuracy of our content, mistakes do happen. If you find a mistake in one of our books—maybe a mistake in the text or the code—we would be grateful if you could report this to us. By doing so, you can save other readers from frustration and help us improve subsequent versions of this book. If you find any errata, please report them by visiting `http://www.packtpub.com/submit-errata`, selecting your book, clicking on the **Errata Submission Form** link, and entering the details of your errata. Once your errata are verified, your submission will be accepted and the errata will be uploaded to our website or added to any list of existing errata under the Errata section of that title.

To view the previously submitted errata, go to `https://www.packtpub.com/books/content/support` and enter the name of the book in the search field. The required information will appear under the **Errata** section.

# Piracy

Piracy of copyrighted material on the Internet is an ongoing problem across all media. At Packt, we take the protection of our copyright and licenses very seriously. If you come across any illegal copies of our works in any form on the Internet, please provide us with the location address or website name immediately so that we can pursue a remedy.

Please contact us at `copyright@packtpub.com` with a link to the suspected pirated material.

We appreciate your help in protecting our authors and our ability to bring you valuable content.

# Questions

If you have a problem with any aspect of this book, you can contact us at `questions@packtpub.com`, and we will do our best to address the problem.

# 1
# Creating Your First Flask Application

*Flask is fun.* This bold declaration is one of the first things you see when you view the official Flask documentation and, over the course of this book, you will come to understand why so many Python developers agree.

In this chapter we shall:

- Briefly discuss the features of the Flask framework
- Set up a development environment and install Flask
- Implement a minimal Flask app and analyze how it works
- Experiment with commonly used APIs and the interactive debugger
- Start working on the blog project that will be progressively enhanced over the course of the book

## What is Flask?

Flask is a lightweight Web framework written in Python. Flask started out as an April fool's joke that became a highly popular underdog in the Python web framework world. It is now one of the most widely used Python web frameworks for start-ups, and is becoming commonly accepted as the perfect tool for quick and simple solutions in most businesses. At its core, it provides a set of powerful libraries for handling the most common web development tasks, such as:

- URL routing that makes it easy to map URLs to your code
- Template rendering with Jinja2, one of the most powerful Python template engines

- Session management and securing cookies
- HTTP request parsing and flexible response handling
- Interactive web-based debugger
- Easy-to-use, flexible application configuration management

This book will teach you how to use these tools through practical, real-world examples. We will also discuss commonly used third-party libraries for things that are not included in Flask, such as database access and form validation. By the end of this book you will be ready to tackle your next big project with Flask.

# With great freedom comes great responsibility

As the documentation states, *Flask is fun*, but it can also be challenging, especially when you are building a large application. Unlike other popular Python web frameworks, such as Django, Flask does not enforce ways of structuring your modules or your code. If you have experience with other web frameworks, you may be surprised how writing applications in Flask feels like writing Python as opposed to the framework boilerplate.

This book will teach you to use Flask to write clean, expressive applications. As you progress through this book, you will not only become a proficient Flask developer but you will also become a stronger Python developer.

# Setting up a development environment

Flask is written in Python, so before we can start writing Flask apps we must ensure that Python is installed. Most Linux distributions and recent versions of OSX come with Python pre-installed. The examples in this book will require Python 2.6 or 2.7. Instructions for installing Python can be found at http://www.python.org.

If this is your first time using Python, there are a number of excellent resources available for free on the web. I would recommend *Learn Python The Hard Way*, by *Zed Shaw*, available for free online at http://learnpythonthehardway.org. Looking for more? You can find a large list of free Python resources at http://resrc.io/list/10/list-of-free-programming-books/#python.

You can verify that Python is installed and that you have the correct version by running the Python interactive interpreter from a command prompt:

```
$ python
Python 2.7.6 (default, Nov 26 2013, 12:52:49)
[GCC 4.8.2] on linux2
Type "help", "copyright", "credits" or "license" for more
information.
>>>
```

At the prompt (>>>) type exit() and hit *Enter* to leave the interpreter.

# Supporting Python 3

This book will include code that is compatible with both Python 2 and Python 3 where possible. Unfortunately, since Python 3 is still relatively new as compared to Python 2, not all third-party packages used in this book are guaranteed to work seamlessly with Python 3. There is a lot of effort being put into making popular open-source libraries compatible with both versions but, at the time of writing, some libraries have still not been ported. For best results, ensure that the version of Python that you have installed on your system is 2.6 or above.

# Installing Python packages

Now that you have ensured that Python is installed correctly, we will install some popular Python packages that will be used over the course of this book.

We will be installing these packages system-wide but, once they are installed, we will be working exclusively in virtual environments.

# Installing pip

The de-facto Python package installer is pip . We will use it throughout the book to install Flask and other third-party libraries.

If you already have setuptools installed, you can install pip by simply running the following command:

```
$ sudo easy_install pip
```

After completing the installation, verify that `pip` is installed correctly:

```
$ pip --version
pip 1.2.1 from /usr/lib/python2.7/site-packages/pip-1.2.1-py2.7.egg
(python 2.7)
```

The version numbers are likely to change, so for a definitive guide please consult the official instructions, which can be found at `http://www.pip-installer.org/en/latest/installing.html`.

# Installing virtualenv

Once pip is installed, we can proceed to install the most important tool in any Python developer's toolkit: `virtualenv`. Virtualenv makes it easy to produce isolated Python environments, complete with their own copies of system and third-party packages.

## Why use virtualenv?

Virtualenv solves a number of problems related to package management. Imagine you have an old application that was built using a very early version of Flask, and you would like to build a new project using the most-recent version of Flask. If Flask was installed system-wide, you was be forced to either upgrade your old project or write your new project against the old Flask. If both projects were using virtualenv, then each could run its own version of Flask, with no conflicts or issues.

Virtualenv makes it easy to control which versions of the third-party package is used by your project.

Another consideration is that installing packages system-wide generally requires elevated privileges (`sudo pip install foo`). By using virtualenvs, you can create Python environments and install packages as a regular user. This is especially useful if you are deploying to a shared hosting environment or are in a situation where you do not have administrator privileges.

## Installing virtualenv with pip

We will use pip to install `virtualenv`; since it is a standard Python package, it can be installed just like any other Python package. To ensure that `virtualenv` is installed system-wide, run the following command (it requires elevated privileges):

```
$ sudo pip install virtualenv
$ virtualenv --version
1.10.1
```

The version numbers are likely to change, so for a definitive guide please consult the official instructions at `http://virtualenv.org`.

# Creating your first Flask app

Now that we have the proper tools installed, we're ready to create our first Flask app. To begin, create a directory somewhere convenient that will hold all of your Python projects. At the command prompt or terminal, navigate to your projects directory; mine is `/home/charles/projects`, or `~/projects` for short on Unix-based systems.

```
$ mkdir ~/projects
$ cd ~/projects
```

Now we will create a `virtualenv`. The commands below will create a new directory named `hello_flask` inside your projects folder that contains a complete, isolated Python environment.

```
$ virtualenv hello_flask

New python executable in hello_flask/bin/python2.

Also creating executable in hello_flask/bin/python

Installing setuptools...........done.

Installing pip..............done.

$ cd hello_flask
```

If you list the contents of the `hello_flask` directory, you will see that it has created several sub-directories, including a `bin` folder (`Scripts` on Windows) that contains copies of both Python and pip. The next step is to activate your new virtualenv. The instructions differ depending on whether you are using Windows or Mac OS/Linux. To activate your virtualenv refer to the following screenshot:

```
@alpha ~ $ cd projects
@alpha projects $ virtualenv hello_flask
New python executable in hello_flask/bin/python2
Also creating executable in hello_flask/bin/python
Installing Setuptools...............................................
.....................................................................
.....................................................................
...done.
Installing Pip.......................................................
.....................................................................
.....................................................................
....................done.
@alpha projects $ cd hello_flask
@alpha hello_flask $ source bin/activate
(hello_flask)@alpha hello_flask $ □
```

Creating the hello_flask virtualenv

When you `activate` a `virtualenv`, your PATH environment variable is temporarily modified to ensure that any packages you install or use are restricted to your `virtualenv`.

# Installing Flask in your virtualenv

Now that we've verified that our `virtualenv` is set up correctly, we can install Flask.

When you are inside a virtualenv, you should never install packages with administrator privileges. If you receive a permission error when attempting to install Flask, double-check that you have activated your `virtualenv` correctly (you should see (`hello_flask`) in your command prompt).

```
(hello_flask) $ pip install Flask
```

You will see some text scroll by as pip downloads the Flask package and the related dependencies before installing it into your virtualenv. Flask depends on a couple of additional third-party libraries, which pip will automatically download and install for you. Let's verify that everything is installed properly:

```
(hello_flask) $ python
>>> import flask
>>> flask.__version__
'0.10.1'
>>> flask
<module 'flask' from
'/home/charles/projects/hello_flask/lib/python2.7/site-
packages/flask/__init__.pyc'>
```

Congratulations! You've installed Flask and now we are ready to start coding.

# Hello, Flask!

Create a new file in the `hello_flask` virtualenv named `app.py`. Using your favorite text editor or IDE, enter the following code:

```
from flask import Flask

app = Flask(__name__)

@app.route('/')
def index():
```

```
        return 'Hello, Flask!'

    if __name__ == '__main__':
        app.run(debug=True)
```

Save the file and then execute `app.py` by running it from the command line. You will need to ensure that you have activated the `hello_flask` virtualenv:

```
$ cd ~/projects/hello_flask
(hello_flask) $ python app.py
* Running on http://127.0.0.1:5000/
```

Open your favorite web-browser and navigate to the URL displayed (`http://127.0.0.1:5000`). You should see the message **Hello, Flask!** displayed on a blank white page. By default, the Flask development server runs locally on `127.0.0.1`, bound to port `5000`.

Your first Flask app.

# Understanding the code

We just created a very basic Flask app. To understand what's happening let's take this code apart line-by-line.

```
from flask import Flask
```

Our app begins by importing the `Flask` class. This class represents a single WSGI application and is the central object in any Flask project.

WSGI is the Python standard web server interface, defined in PEP 333. You can think of WSGI as a set of behaviors and methods that, when implemented, allow your web app to just work with a large number of webservers. Flask handles all the implementation details for you, so you can focus on writing you web app.

```
app = Flask(__name__)
```

In this line, we create an application instance in the variable `app` and pass it the name of our module. The variable `app` can of course be anything, however `app` is a common convention for most Flask applications. The application instance is the central registry for things such as views, URL routes, template configuration, and much more. We provide the name of the current module so that the application is able to find resources by looking inside the current folder. This will be important later when we want to render templates or serve static files.

```
@app.route('/')
def index():
    return 'Hello, Flask!'
```

In the preceding lines, we are instructing our Flask app to route all requests for / (the root URL) to this view function (`index`). A view is simply a function or a method that returns a response of some kind. Whenever you open a browser and navigate to the root URL of our app, Flask will call this view function and send the return value to the browser.

There are a few things to note about these lines of code:

- `@app.route` is a Python decorator from the `app` variable defined above. This decorator (`app.route`) wraps the following function, in this case,`index`, in order to route requests for a particular URL to a particular view. Index is chosen as the name for the function here, as it's the common name for the first page that a web server uses. Other examples could be homepage or main. Decorators are a rich and interesting subject for Python developers, so if you are not familiar with them, I recommend using your favorite search engine to find a good tutorial.

- The `index` function takes no arguments. This might seem odd if you are coming from other web-frameworks and were expecting a request object or something similar. We will see in the following examples how to access values from the request.

- The `index` function returns a plain string object. In later examples, we will see how to render templates to return HTML.

- The following lines execute our app using the built-in development server in debug mode. The 'if' statement is a common Python convention that ensures that the app will only be run when we run our script via python `app.py`, and will not run if we try to import this app from another Python file.

```
if __name__ == '__main__':
    app.run(debug=True)
```

# Routes and requests

Right now our Flask app isn't much fun, so let's look at the different ways in which we can add more interesting behavior to our web app. One common way is to add responsive behavior so that our app will look at values in the URL and handle them. Let's add a new route to our Hello Flask app called `hello`. This new route will display a greeting to the person whose name appears in the URL:

```python
from flask import Flask

app = Flask(__name__)

@app.route('/')
def index():
    return 'Hello, Flask!'

@app.route('/hello/<name>')
def hello(name):
    return 'Hello, %s' % name

if __name__ == '__main__':
    app.run(debug=True)
```

Again, let's run our app and open it up in a web browser. We can now navigate to a URL such as `http://127.0.0.1/hello/Charlie` and see our custom message:

Our Flask app displaying a custom message

In the preceding example, the route we added specifies a single parameter: `name`. This parameter also appears in the function declaration as the sole argument. Flask is automatically matching the URL `/hello/Charlie` to the `hello` view; this is known as mapping. It then passes the string `Charlie` into our view function as an argument.

What happens if we navigate to `http://127.0.0.1:5000/hello/` without specifying a name? As you can see, the Flask development server will return a 404 response, indicating that the URL did not match any known routes.

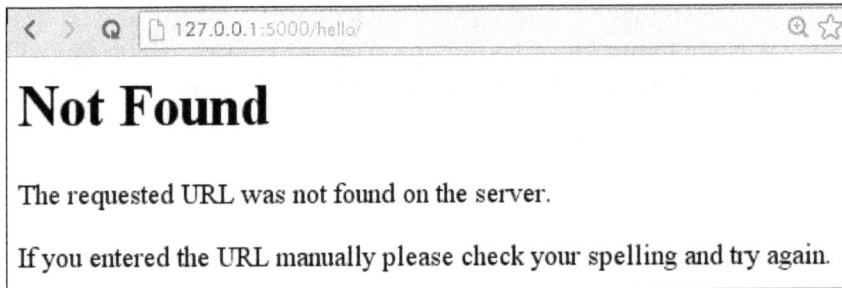

Flask 404 page

# Reading values from the request

In addition to the URL, values can be passed to your app in the query string. The query string is made up of arbitrary keys and values that are tacked onto the URL, using a question-mark:

| URL | Argument Values |
|-----|-----------------|
| `/hello/?name=Charlie` | name: Charlie |
| `/hello/?name=Charlie&favorite_color=green` | name: Charlie<br>favorite_color: green |

In order to access these values inside your view functions, Flask provides a request object that encapsulates all sorts of information about the current HTTP request. In the following example, we will modify our `hello` view to also respond to names passed in via the query string. If no name is specified either on the query-string or in the URL, we will return a 404.

```
from flask import Flask, abort, request

app = Flask(__name__)

@app.route('/')
def index():
    return 'Hello, Flask!'

@app.route('/hello/<name>')
@app.route('/hello/')
def hello(name=None):
```

```
    if name is None:
        # If no name is specified in the URL, attempt to retrieve it
        # from the query string.
        name = request.args.get('name')
        if name:
            return 'Hello, %s' % name
    else:
        # No name was specified in the URL or the query string.
        abort(404)

if __name__ == '__main__':
    app.run(debug=True)
```

As you can see, we have added another route decorator to our `hello` view: Flask allows you to map multiple URL routes to the same view. Because our new route does not contain a name parameter, we need to modify the argument signature of our view function to make `name` an optional parameter, which we accomplish by providing a default value of `None`.

The function body of our view has also been modified to check for the presence of a name in the URL. If no name is specified, we will abort with a `404` page not found status code.

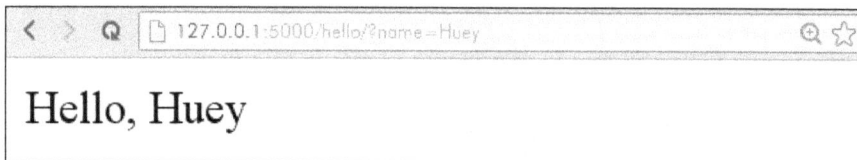

Greet someone using the query string

# Debugging Flask applications

It is inevitable that, sooner or later, we will introduce a bug into our code. Since bugs are inevitable, the best thing we can hope for as developers is good tools that help us diagnose and fix bugs quickly. Luckily, Flask comes bundled with an extremely powerful web-based debugger. The Flask debugger makes it possible to introspect the state of your application the moment an error occurs, removing the need to sprinkle in print statements or breakpoints.

This can be enabled by telling the Flask app to run in `debug` mode at run time. We can do this in a few ways but we have actually already done this through the following code:

```
if __name__ == '__main__':
    app.run(debug=True)
```

In order to try it out, let's introduce a bug to the `hello_flask` app by creating a typo. Here I have simply deleted the trailing e from the variable `name`:

```python
@app.route('/hello/<name>')
@app.route('/hello/')
def hello(name=None):
    if nam is None:
        # No name was specified in the URL or the query string.
        abort(404)
```

When we fire up the development server and attempt to access our view, we are now presented with the debugging page:

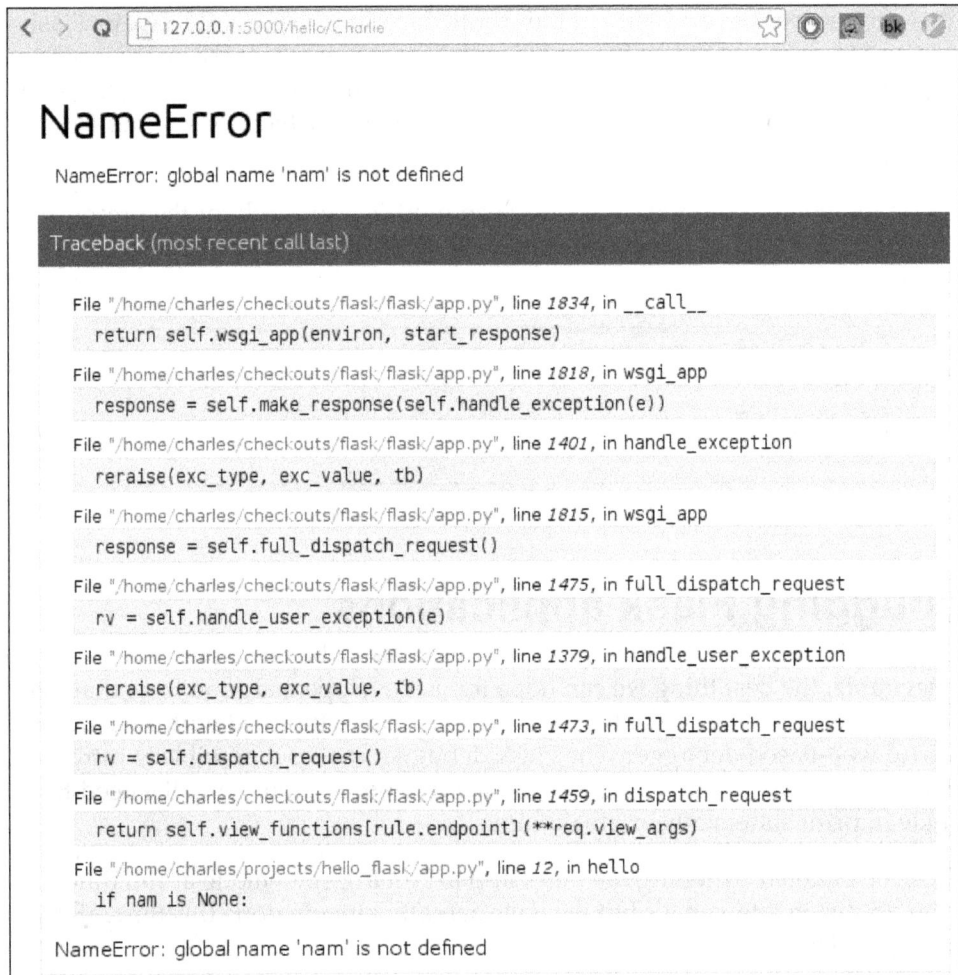

The Flask interactive debugger running in a web browser

This list of code is called a **Traceback** and it is made up of the call stack, the nested list of function calls that preceded the actual error. The traceback usually provides a very good clue as to what may have happened. At the very bottom we see the line of code we intentionally mistyped along with the actual Python error, which is a **NameError** exception telling us that **nam** is not defined.

```
File "/home/charles/projects/hello_flask/app.py", line 12, in hello
    if nam is None:

NameError: global name 'nam' is not defined
```

Traceback detail showing our typo and a description of the error

The real magic happens when you place your mouse on the highlighted line with the mouse. On the right-hand side you will see two small icons representing a terminal and a source code file. Clicking the **Source Code** icon will expand the source code surrounding the line that contained the error. This is very useful for establishing some context when interpreting an error.

The terminal icon is the most interesting. When you click the **Terminal** icon, a small console appears with the standard Python prompt. This prompt allows you to inspect, in real-time, the values of the local variables at the time of the exception. Try typing in name and hitting *Enter*—it should display the value, if any, that was specified in the URL. We can also introspect the current request arguments as follows:

```
File "/home/charles/projects/hello_flask/app.py", line 12, in hello
  if nam is None:

[console ready]
>>> name
u'Charlie'
>>> request.args
werkzeug.datastructures.ImmutableMultiDict({})
>>>
```

Introspecting variables using the debugging console

As you work through the chapters and experiment on your own, being able to quickly diagnose and correct any bugs will be an extremely valuable skill. We will return to the interactive debugger in *Chapter 8, Testing Flask Apps* but, for now, be aware that it exists and can be used to introspect your code when and where it breaks.

# Introducing the blog project

Over the rest of this book, we will be building, enhancing, and deploying a programmer-friendly blogging site. This project will introduce you to the most common web development tasks, such as working with relational databases, processing and validating form data, and (everyone's favorite), testing. In each chapter, you will learn a new skill through practical, hands-on coding projects. In the following table, I've listed a brief description of the core skills paired with the corresponding features of the blog:

| Skill | Blog site feature(s) |
|---|---|
| Relational databases with SQLAlchemy<br><br>Flask-SQLAlchemy | Store entries and tags in a relational database. Perform a wide variety of queries, including pagination, date-ranges, full-text search, inner and outer joins, and more. |
| Form processing and validation<br><br>Flask-WTF | Create and edit blog entries using forms. In later chapters, we will also use forms for logging users into the site and allowing visitors to post comments. |
| Template rendering with Jinja2<br><br>Jinja2 | Create a clean, extensible set of templates, making use of inheritance and includes, where appropriate. |
| User authentication and administrative dashboards<br><br>Flask-Login | Store user accounts in the database and restrict the post management page to registered users. Build an administrative panel for managing posts, user accounts, and for displaying stats such as page-views, IP geolocation, and more. |
| Ajax and RESTful APIs<br><br>Flask-API | Build an Ajax-powered commenting system that will be displayed on each entry. Expose blog entries using a RESTful API, and build a simple command-line client for posting entries using the API. |
| Unit testing<br><br>unittest | We will build a full suite of tests for the blog, and learn how to simulate real requests and use mocks to simplify complex interactions. |
| Everything else | **Cross-Site Request Forgery (CSRF)** protection, Atom feeds, spam detection, asynchronous task execution, deploying, **Secure Socket Layer (SSL)**, hosting providers, and more. |

# The spec

It's always a good idea when starting a large project to have a functional specification in mind. For the blogging site, our spec will simply be the list of features that we want our blog to have. These features are based on my experience in building my personal blog:

- Entries should be entered using web-based interfaces. For formatting, the author can use **Markdown**, a lightweight, visually appealing markup language.

- Images can be uploaded to the site and easily embedded in blog entries.

- Entries can be organized using any number of tags.

- The site should support multiple authors.

- Entries can be displayed in order of publication, but also listed by month, by tag, or by author. Long lists of entries will be paginated.

- Entries can be saved as *drafts* and viewed by their author but nobody else until they are *published*.

- Visitors to the site can post comments on entries, which will be checked for spam and then left to the author's discretion as to whether they should remain visible.

- Atom feeds will be made available for all posts, including separate feeds for each author and tag.

- Entries can be accessed using a RESTful API. Authors will be given an API token that will allow them to modify entries using the API.

While this list is not exhaustive, it covers the core functionality of our blogging site and you will hopefully find it both fun and challenging to build. At the end of the book, I will present some ideas for additional features that you might add, but first you need to become comfortable working with Flask. I'm sure you're eager to get started, so let's set up our blogging project.

# Creating the blog project

Let's start by creating a new project within our working directory; on my laptop this is /home/charles/projects, or on a Unix system ~/projects, for short. This is exactly what we did when we created the hello_flask app:

```
$ cd ~/projects
$ mkdir blog
$ cd blog
```

We will then need to set up our `virtualenv` environment. This differs from what we did earlier as this is a more structured way of using virtualenv:

```
$ virtualenv blog
```

The next step will be to install Flask into our virtualenv. To do this, we will `activate` the `virtualenv` and use `pip` to install Flask:

```
$ source blog/bin/activate
(blog) $ pip install Flask
```

Up until now, all of this should be somewhat familiar to you. However, instead of creating a single file for our app, which we are definitely allowed to do and that makes sense for very small apps, we can also create a new folder named `app` that will allow us to make our app modular and more logical. Inside that folder, we will create five empty files named `__init__.py`, `app.py`, `config.py`, `main.py`, and `views.py` as follows:

```
mkdir app
touch app/{__init__,app,config,main,views}.py
```

This last command uses a little trick of your shell to create multiple files with the names within the brackets. If you use version control, you will want to treat the `app` directory as the root of your repository. The app directory will contain the source code, templates, and static assets for the blog app. If you haven't used version control, now would be a great time to give it a try. *Pro Git* is a great resource and is available for free at `http://git-scm.com/book`.

What are these files that we just created? As you will see, each file serves an important purpose. Hopefully their names provide a clue as to their purpose, but here is a brief overview of each module's responsibility:

| `__init__.py` | Tells Python to use the app/ directory as a python package |
|---|---|
| `app.py` | The Flask app |
| `config.py` | Configuration variables for our Flask app |
| `main.py` | Entry-point for executing our application |
| `views.py` | URL routes and views for the app |

# A barebones Flask app

Let's fill in these files with the minimum amount of code needed to create a runnable Flask app. This will get our project in good shape for the second chapter, in which we'll start working on the code to store and retrieve blog entries from the database.

We will start with the config.py module. This module will contain a Configuration class that instructs Flask that we want to run our app in the DEBUG mode. Add the following two lines of code to the config.py module as follows:

```
class Configuration(object):
    DEBUG = True
```

Next we will create our Flask app and instruct it to use the configuration values specified in the config module. Add the following code to the app.py module:

```
from flask import Flask

from config import Configuration  # import our configuration data.

app = Flask(__name__)
app.config.from_object(Configuration)  # use values from our
Configuration object.
```

The views module will contain a single view mapped to the root URL of the site. Add the following code to views.py:

```
from app import app

@app.route('/')
def homepage():
    return 'Home page'
```

As you probably noticed, we are still missing our call to app.run(). We will put that code in main.py, which we will use as the entry-point into our app. Add the following code to the main.py module:

```
from app import app  # import our Flask app
import views

if __name__ == '__main__':
    app.run()
```

We do not call app.run(debug=True) because we have already instructed Flask to run our app in the debug mode in the Configuration object.

You can run the app from the command-line by executing the `main` module as follows:

```
$ python main.py
 * Running on http://127.0.0.1:5000/
* Restarting with reloader
```

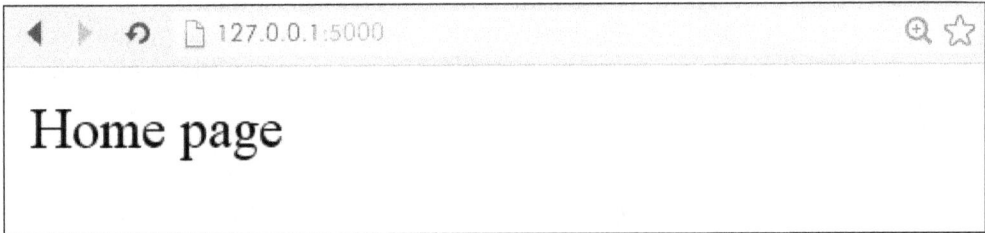

From humble beginnings...

## Zooming out

Other than the `Configuration` class, most of this code should look familiar to you. We have basically taken the code from the `hello_flask` example and separated it into several modules. It may seem silly to write only two or three lines of code per file, but as our project grows you will see how this early commitment to organization pays off.

You may have noticed that there is an internal prioritization to these files, based on the order in which they are imported—this is to mitigate the possibility of a circular import. A circular import occurs when two modules mutually import each other and, hence, cannot be imported at all. When using the Flask framework, it is very easy to create circular imports because so many different things depend on the central app object. To avoid problems, some people just put everything into a single module. This works fine for smaller apps, but is not maintainable beyond a certain size or complexity. That is why we have broken our app into several modules and created a single entry-point that controls the ordering of imports.

# The import flow

Execution starts when you run python `main.py` from the command line. The first line of code that the Python interpreter runs into imports the `app` object from the `app` module. Now we're inside `app.py`, which imports Flask and our `Configuration` object. The rest of the `app.py` module is read and interpreted, and we're back into `main.py` again. The second line of `main.py` imports the `views` module. Now we're in `views.py`, which depends on `app.py` for `@app.route` and is, in fact, already available from `main.py`. The URL route and view are registered as the `views` module is interpreted, and we're back into `main.py` again. Since we are running `main.py` directly, the 'if' check will evaluate to `True` and our app will run.

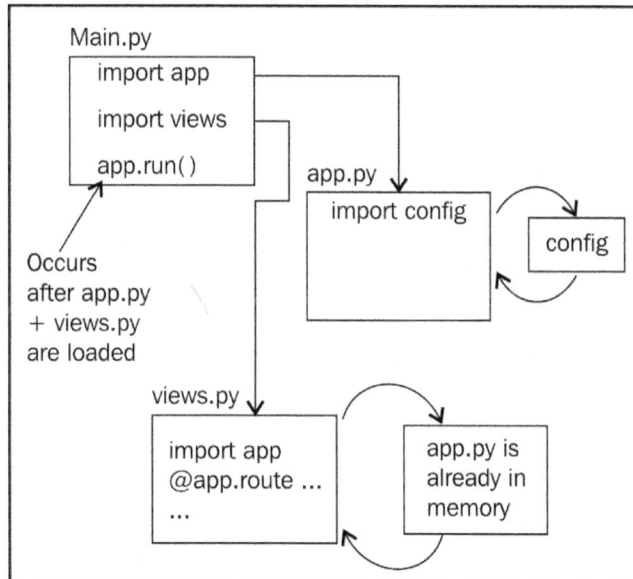

Import flow when executing main.py

# Summary

By now you should be familiar with the process of setting up a new virtualenv for your Python project, be able to install Flask, and have created a simple app. In this chapter,we discussed how to create virtualenvs for your projects and install third-party packages using `pip`. We also learnt how to write a basic Flask app, route requests to views, and to read request arguments. We familiarized ourselves with the interactive debugger and with how the Python interpreter processes the import statements.

If you were already familiar with most of the subject-matter in this chapter, do not worry; things will soon get more challenging.

In the next chapter, you will discover how to work with a relational database to store and retrieve blog entries. We'll add a new module to our project for storing our database-specific code and create some models to represent blog entries and tags. Once we are able to store the entries, we will learn how to read them back in a variety of ways through filtering, sorting, and aggregation. For more information, you can refer to the following links:

- `https://www.python.org/dev/peps/pep-0333/`
- `https://wiki.python.org/moin/PythonDecorators`
- `http://charlesleifer.com`

# 2
# Relational Databases with SQLAlchemy

Relational databases are the bedrock upon which almost every modern Web application is built. Learning to think about your application in terms of tables and relationships is one of the keys to a clean, well-designed project. As you will see in this chapter, the data model you choose early on will affect almost every facet of the code that follows. We will be using SQLAlchemy, a powerful object relational mapper that allows us to abstract away the complexities of multiple database engines, to work with the database directly from within Python.

In this chapter, we shall:

- Present a brief overview of the benefits of using a relational database
- Introduce SQLAlchemy, the Python SQL Toolkit and Object Relational Mapper
- Configure our Flask application to use SQLAlchemy
- Write a model class to represent blog entries
- Learn how to save and retrieve blog entries from the database
- Perform queries – sorting, filtering, and aggregation
- Build a tagging system for blog entries
- Create schema migrations using Alembic

# Why use a relational database?

Our application's database is much more than a simple record of things that we need to save for future retrieval. If all we needed to do was save and retrieve data, we could easily use flat text files. The fact is, though, that we want to be able to perform interesting queries on our data. What's more, we want to do this efficiently and without reinventing the wheel. While non-relational databases (sometimes known as NoSQL databases) are very popular and have their place in the world of the web, relational databases long ago solved the common problems of filtering, sorting, aggregating, and joining tabular data. Relational databases allow us to define sets of data in a structured way that maintains the consistency of our data. Using relational databases also gives us, the developers, the freedom to focus on the parts of our app that matter.

In addition to efficiently performing ad hoc queries, a relational database server will also do the following:

- Ensure that our data conforms to the rules set forth in the schema
- Allow multiple people to access the database concurrently, while at the same time guaranteeing the consistency of the underlying data
- Ensure that data, once saved, is not lost even in the event of an application crash

Relational databases and SQL, the programming language used with relational databases, are topics worthy of an entire book. Because this book is devoted to teaching you how to build apps with Flask, I will show you how to use a tool that has been widely adopted by the Python community for working with databases, namely, SQLAlchemy.

> SQLAlchemy abstracts away many of the complications of writing SQL queries, but there is no substitute for a deep understanding of SQL and the relational model. For that reason, if you are new to SQL, I would recommend that you check out the colorful book *Learn SQL the Hard Way, Zed Shaw* available online for free at http://sql.learncodethehardway.org/.

# Introducing SQLAlchemy

SQLAlchemy is an extremely powerful library for working with relational databases in Python. Instead of writing SQL queries by hand, we can use normal Python objects to represent database tables and execute queries. There are a number of benefits to this approach, as follows:

- Your application can be developed entirely in Python.

- Subtle differences between database engines are abstracted away. This allows you to do things just like a lightweight database, for instance, use SQLite for local development and testing, then switch to the databases designed for high loads (such as PostgreSQL) in production.

- Database errors are less common because there are now two layers between your application and the database server: the Python interpreter itself (this will catch the obvious syntax errors), and SQLAlchemy, which has well-defined APIs and its own layer of error-checking.

- Your database code may become more efficient, thanks to SQLAlchemy's unit-of-work model that helps reduce unnecessary round-trips to the database. SQLAlchemy also has facilities for efficiently pre-fetching related objects known as eager loading.

- **Object Relational Mapping (ORM)** makes your code more maintainable, an aspiration known as **don't repeat yourself**, (**DRY**). Suppose you add a column to a model. With SQLAlchemy it will be available whenever you use that model. If, on the other hand, you had hand-written SQL queries strewn throughout your app, you would need to update each query, one at a time, to ensure that you were including the new column.

- SQLAlchemy can help you avoid SQL injection vulnerabilities.

- Excellent library support: As you will see in later chapters, there are a multitude of useful libraries that can work directly with your SQLAlchemy models to provide things such as maintenance interfaces and RESTful APIs.

I hope you're excited after reading this list. If all the items in this list don't make sense to you right now, don't worry. As you work through this chapter and the subsequent ones, these benefits will become more apparent and meaningful.

Now that we have discussed some of the benefits of using SQLAlchemy, let's install it and start coding.

> If you'd like to learn more about SQLAlchemy, there is a chapter devoted entirely to its design in *The Architecture of Open-Source Applications*, available online for free at http://aosabook.org/en/sqlalchemy.html.

# Installing SQLAlchemy

We will use `pip` to install SQLAlchemy into the blog app's virtualenv. As you will recall from the previous chapter, to activate your virtualenv, change directories to `source` the `activate` script as follows:

```
$ cd ~/projects/blog
$ source blog/bin/activate
(blog) $ pip install sqlalchemy
Downloading/unpacking sqlalchemy
...
Successfully installed sqlalchemy
Cleaning up...
```

You can check if your installation succeeded by opening a Python interpreter and checking the SQLAlchemy version; note that your exact version number is likely to differ.

```
$ python
>>> import sqlalchemy
>>> sqlalchemy.__version__
'0.9.0b2'
```

# Using SQLAlchemy in our Flask app

SQLAlchemy works very well with Flask on its own, but the author of Flask has released a special Flask extension named **Flask-SQLAlchemy** that provides helpers with many common tasks, and can save us from having to re-invent the wheel later on. Let's use `pip` to install this extension:

```
(blog) $ pip install flask-sqlalchemy
...
Successfully installed flask-sqlalchemy
```

Flask provides a standard interface for the developers who are interested in building extensions. As the framework has grown in popularity, the number of high-quality extensions has increased. If you'd like to take a look at some of the more popular extensions, there is a curated list available on the Flask project website at `http://flask.pocoo.org/extensions/`.

# Choosing a database engine

SQLAlchemy supports a multitude of popular database dialects, including SQLite, MySQL, and PostgreSQL. Depending on the database you would like to use, you may need to install an additional Python package containing a database driver. Listed next are several popular databases supported by SQLAlchemy and the corresponding pip-installable driver. Some databases have multiple driver options, so I have listed the most popular one first.

| Database | Driver Package(s) |
| --- | --- |
| SQLite | Not needed, part of the Python standard library since version 2.5 |
| MySQL | MySQL-python, PyMySQL (pure Python), OurSQL |
| PostgreSQL | psycopg2 |
| Firebird | fdb |
| Microsoft SQL Server | pymssql, PyODBC |
| Oracle | cx-Oracle |

SQLite comes as standard with Python and does not require a separate server process, so it is perfect for getting up-and-running quickly. For simplicity in the examples that follow, I will demonstrate how to configure the blog app for use with SQLite. If you have a different database in mind that you would like to use for the blog project, feel free to use `pip` to install the necessary driver package at this time.

# Connecting to the database

Using your favorite text editor, open the `config.py` module for our blog project (`~/projects/blog/app/config.py`). We are going to add a SQLAlchemy-specific setting to instruct Flask-SQLAlchemy how to connect to our database. The new lines are highlighted in the following:

```
import os
class Configuration(object):
    APPLICATION_DIR = os.path.dirname(os.path.realpath(__file__))
    DEBUG = True
    SQLALCHEMY_DATABASE_URI = 'sqlite:///%s/blog.db' % APPLICATION_DIR
```

The SQLALCHEMY_DATABASE_URI comprises the following parts:

```
dialect+driver://username:password@host:port/database
```

Because SQLite databases are stored in local files, the only information we need to provide is the path to the database file. On the other hand, if you wanted to connect to PostgreSQL running locally, your URI might look something like this:

```
postgresql://postgres:secretpassword@localhost:5432/blog_db
```

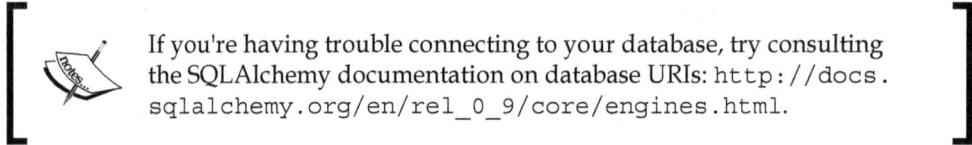

> If you're having trouble connecting to your database, try consulting the SQLAlchemy documentation on database URIs: http://docs.sqlalchemy.org/en/rel_0_9/core/engines.html.

Now that we've specified how to connect to the database, let's create the object responsible for actually managing our database connections. This object is provided by the Flask-SQLAlchemy extension and is conveniently named SQLAlchemy. Open app.py and make the following additions:

```
from flask import Flask
from flask.ext.sqlalchemy import SQLAlchemy

from config import Configuration

app = Flask(__name__)
app.config.from_object(Configuration)
db = SQLAlchemy(app)
```

These changes instruct our Flask app, and in turn SQLAlchemy, how to communicate with our application's database. The next step will be to create a table for storing blog entries and, to do so, we will create our first model.

# Creating the Entry model

A **model** is the data representation of a table of data that we want to store in the database. These models have attributes called **columns** that represent the data items in the data. So, if we were creating a Person model, we might have columns for storing the first and last name, date of birth, home address, hair color, and so on. Since we are interested in creating a model to represent blog entries, we will have columns for things like the title and body content.

[ ✏ Note that we don't say a `People` model or `Entries` model –
models are singular even though they commonly represent many
different objects. ]

With SQLAlchemy, creating a model is as easy as defining a class and specifying a
number of attributes assigned to that class. Let's start with a very basic model for our
blog entries. Create a new file named `models.py` in the blog project's `app/` directory
and enter the following code:

```python
import datetime, re

from app import db

def slugify(s):
    return re.sub('[^\w]+', '-', s).lower()

class Entry(db.Model):
    id = db.Column(db.Integer, primary_key=True)
    title = db.Column(db.String(100))
    slug = db.Column(db.String(100), unique=True)
    body = db.Column(db.Text)
    created_timestamp = db.Column(db.DateTime, default=datetime.
datetime.now)
    modified_timestamp = db.Column(
        db.DateTime,
        default=datetime.datetime.now,
        onupdate=datetime.datetime.now)

    def __init__(self, *args, **kwargs):
        super(Entry, self).__init__(*args, **kwargs)  # Call parent
constructor.
        self.generate_slug()

    def generate_slug(self):
        self.slug = ''
        if self.title:
            self.slug = slugify(self.title)

    def __repr__(self):
        return '<Entry: %s>' % self.title
```

There is a lot going on, so let's start with the imports and work our way down. We begin by importing the standard library datetime and re modules. We will be using datetime to get the current date and time, and re to do some string manipulation. The next import statement brings in the db object that we created in app.py. As you recall, the db object is an instance of the SQLAlchemy class, which is a part of the Flask-SQLAlchemy extension. The db object provides access to the classes that we need to construct our Entry model, which is just a few lines ahead.

Before the Entry model, we define a helper function slugify, which we will use to give our blog entries some nice URLs (used in *Chapter 3, Templates and Views*). The slugify function takes a string such as *A post about Flask* and uses a regular expression to turn a string that is human-readable in to a URL, and so returns *a-post-about-flask*.

Next is the Entry model. Our Entry model is a normal class that extends db.Model. By extending db.Model, our Entry class will inherit a variety of helpers that we'll use to query the database.

The attributes of the Entry model, are a simple mapping of the names and data that we wish to store in the database and are listed as follows:

- id: This is the primary key for our database table. This value is set for us automatically by the database when we create a new blog entry, usually an auto-incrementing number for each new entry. While we will not explicitly set this value, a primary key comes in handy when you want to refer one model to another, as you'll see later in the chapter.

- title: The title for a blog entry, stored as a String column with a maximum length of 100.

- slug: The URL-friendly representation of the title, stored as a String column with a maximum length of 100. This column also specifies unique=True, so that no two entries can share the same slug.

- body: The actual content of the post, stored in a Text column. This differs from the String type of the Title and Slug as you can store as much text as you like in this field.

- created_timestamp: The time a blog entry was created, stored in a DateTime column. We instruct SQLAlchemy to automatically populate this column with the current time by default when an entry is first saved.

- modified_timestamp: The time a blog entry was last updated. SQLAlchemy will automatically update this column with the current time whenever we save an entry.

> For short strings such as titles or names of things, the `String` column is appropriate, but when the text may be especially long it is better to use a `Text` column, as we did for the entry body.

We've overridden the constructor for the class (`__init__`) so that, when a new model is created, it automatically sets the slug for us based on the title.

The last piece is the `__repr__` method that is used to generate a helpful representation of instances of our `Entry` class. The specific meaning of `__repr__` is not important but allows you to reference the object that the program is working with, when debugging.

A final bit of code needs to be added to main.py, the entry-point to our application, to ensure that the models are imported. Add the highlighted changes to main.py as follows:

```
from app import app, db
import models
import views

if __name__ == '__main__':
    app.run()
```

# Creating the Entry table

In order to start working with the `Entry` model, we first need to create a table for it in our database. Luckily, Flask-SQLAlchemy comes with a nice helper for doing just this. Create a new sub-folder named `scripts` in the blog project's app directory. Then create a file named `create_db.py`:

```
(blog) $ cd app/
(blog) $ mkdir scripts
(blog) $ touch scripts/create_db.py
```

Add the following code to the `create_db.py` module. This function will automatically look at all the code that we have written and create a new table in our database for the `Entry` model based on our models:

```
import os, sys
sys.path.append(os.getcwd())
from main import db

if __name__ == '__main__':
    db.create_all()
```

Execute the script from inside the `app/` directory. Make sure the virtualenv is active. If everything goes successfully, you should see no output.

```
(blog) $ python create_db.py
(blog) $
```

> If you encounter errors while creating the database tables, make sure you are in the app directory, with the virtualenv activated, when you run the script. Next, ensure that there are no typos in your SQLALCHEMY_DATABASE_URI setting.

# Working with the Entry model

Let's experiment with our new `Entry` model by saving a few blog entries. We will be doing this from the Python interactive shell. At this stage let's install **IPython**, a sophisticated shell with features such as tab-completion (that the default Python shell lacks).

```
(blog) $ pip install ipython
```

Now check whether we are in the `app` directory and let's start the shell and create a couple of entries as follows:

```
(blog) $ ipython
```

```
In []: from models import *  # First things first, import our Entry model
and db object.
In []: db  # What is db?
Out[]: <SQLAlchemy engine='sqlite:////home/charles/projects/blog/app/
blog.db'>
```

> If you are familiar with the normal Python shell but not IPython, things may look a little different at first. The main thing to be aware of is that In [] refers to the code you type in, and Out [] is the output of the commands you put into the shell.

IPython has a neat feature that allows you to print detailed information about an object. This is done by typing in the object's name followed by a question-mark (?). Introspecting the `Entry` model provides a bit of information, including the argument signature and the string representing that object (known as the `docstring`) of the constructor.

```
In []: Entry?  # What is Entry and how do we create it?
Type:        _BoundDeclarativeMeta
String Form:<class 'models.Entry'>
File:        /home/charles/projects/blog/app/models.py
Docstring:   <no docstring>
Constructor information:
 Definition:Entry(self, *args, **kwargs)
```

We can create `Entry` objects by passing column values in as the keyword-arguments. In the preceding example, it uses **kwargs; this is a shortcut for taking a `dict` object and using it as the values for defining the object, as shown next:

```
In []: first_entry = Entry(title='First entry', body='This is the body of
my first entry.')
```

In order to save our first entry, we will to add it to the database session. The session is simply an object that represents our actions on the database. Even after adding it to the session, it will not be saved to the database yet. In order to save the entry to the database, we need to commit our session:

```
In []: db.session.add(first_entry)
In []: first_entry.id is None  # No primary key, the entry has not been
saved.
Out[]: True
In []: db.session.commit()
In []: first_entry.id
Out[]: 1
In []: first_entry.created_timestamp
Out[]: datetime.datetime(2014, 1, 25, 9, 49, 53, 1337)
```

As you can see from the preceding code examples, once we commit the session, a unique id will be assigned to our first entry and the `created_timestamp` will be set to the current time. Congratulations, you've created your first blog entry!

Try adding a few more on your own. You can add multiple entry objects to the same session before committing, so give that a try as well.

> At any point while you are experimenting, feel free to delete the
> `blog.db` file and re-run the `create_db.py` script to start over
> with a fresh database.

# Making changes to an existing entry

In order to make changes to an existing `Entry`, simply make your edits and then
commit. Let's retrieve our `Entry` using the id that was returned to us earlier, make
some changes, and commit it. SQLAlchemy will know that it needs to be updated.
Here is how you might make edits to the first entry:

```
In []: first_entry = Entry.query.get(1)
In []: first_entry.body = 'This is the first entry, and I have made some
edits.'
In []: db.session.commit()
```

And just like that your changes are saved.

# Deleting an entry

Deleting an entry is just as easy as creating one. Instead of calling `db.session.`
`add`, we will call `db.session.delete` and pass in the `Entry` instance that we wish
to remove.

```
In []: bad_entry = Entry(title='bad entry', body='This is a lousy
entry.')
In []: db.session.add(bad_entry)
In []: db.session.commit()  # Save the bad entry to the database.
In []: db.session.delete(bad_entry)
In []: db.session.commit()  # The bad entry is now deleted from the
database.
```

# Retrieving blog entries

While creating, updating, and deleting are fairly straightforward operations, the real
fun starts when we look at ways to retrieve our entries. We'll start with the basics,
and then work our way up to more interesting queries.

We will use a special attribute on our model class to make queries: `Entry.query`.
This attribute exposes a variety of APIs for working with the collection of entries in
the database.

Let's simply retrieve a list of all the entries in the `Entry` table:

```
In []: entries = Entry.query.all()
In []: entries  # What are our entries?
Out[]: [<Entry u'First entry'>, <Entry u'Second entry'>, <Entry
u'Third entry'>, <Entry u'Fourth entry'>]
```

As you can see, in this example the query returns a list of `Entry` instances that we created. When no explicit ordering is specified, the entries are returned to us in an arbitrary order chosen by the database. Let's specify that we want the entries returned to us in an alphabetical order by title:

```
In []: Entry.query.order_by(Entry.title.asc()).all()
Out []:
[<Entry u'First entry'>,
 <Entry u'Fourth entry'>,
 <Entry u'Second entry'>,
 <Entry u'Third entry'>]
```

Shown next is how you would list your entries in reverse-chronological order, based on when they were last updated:

```
In []: oldest_to_newest = Entry.query.order_by(Entry.modified_timestamp.
desc()).all()
Out []:
[<Entry: Fourth entry>,
 <Entry: Third entry>,
 <Entry: Second entry>,
 <Entry: First entry>]
```

# Filtering the list of entries

It is very useful to be able to retrieve the entire collection of blog entries, but what if we want to filter the list? We could always retrieve the entire collection and then filter it in Python using a loop, but that would be very inefficient. Instead we will rely on the database to do the filtering for us, and simply specify the conditions for which entries should be returned. In the following example, we will specify that we want to filter by entries where the title equals `'First entry'`.

```
In []: Entry.query.filter(Entry.title == 'First entry').all()
Out[]: [<Entry u'First entry'>]
```

If this seems somewhat magical to you, it's because it really is! SQLAlchemy uses operator overloading to convert expressions such as `<Model>.<column> == <some value>` into an abstracted object called `BinaryExpression`. When you are ready to execute your query, these data-structures are then translated into SQL.

> A `BinaryExpression` is simply an object that represents the logical comparison and is produced by over riding the standards methods that are typically called on an object when comparing values in Python.

In order to retrieve a single entry, you have two options: `.first()` and `.one()`. Their differences and similarities are summarized in the following table:

| Number of matching rows | first() behavior | one() behavior |
| --- | --- | --- |
| 1 | Return the object | Return the object |
| 0 | Return None | Raise sqlalchemy.orm. exc.NoResultFound |
| 2+ | Return the first object (based on either explicit ordering or the ordering chosen by the database) | Raise sqlalchemy. orm.exc. MultipleResultsFound |

Let's try the same query as before but, instead of calling `.all()`, we will call `.first()` to retrieve a single `Entry` instance:

```
In []: Entry.query.filter(Entry.title == 'First entry').first()
Out[]: <Entry u'First entry'>
```

Notice how previously `.all()` returned a list containing the object, whereas `.first()` returned just the object itself.

# Special lookups

In the previous example we tested for equality, but there are many other types of lookups possible. In the following table, we have listed some that you may find useful. A complete list can be found in the SQLAlchemy documentation.

| Example | Meaning |
| --- | --- |
| Entry.title == 'The title' | Entries where the title is "The title", case-sensitive. |
| Entry.title != 'The title' | Entries where the title is not "The title". |
| Entry.created_timestamp < datetime.date(2014, 1, 25) | Entries created before January 25, 2014. For less than or equal, use <=. |
| Entry.created_timestamp > datetime.date(2014, 1, 25) | Entries created after January 25, 2014. For greater than or equal, use >=. |
| Entry.body.contains('Python') | Entries where the body contains the word "Python", case-sensitive. |
| Entry.title.endswith('Python') | Entries where the title ends with the string "Python", case-sensitive. Note that this will also match titles that end with the word "CPython", for example. |
| Entry.title.startswith('Python') | Entries where the title starts with the string "Python", case-sensitive. Note that this will also match titles such as "Pythonistas". |
| Entry.body.ilike('%python%') | Entries where the body contains the word "python" anywhere in the text, case-insensitive. The "%" character is a wild card. |
| Entry.title.in_(['Title one', 'Title two']) | Entries where the title is in the given list, either 'Title one' or 'Title two'. |

# Combining expressions

The expressions listed in the preceding table can be combined using bitwise operators to produce arbitrarily complex expressions. Let's say we want to retrieve all blog entries that have the word Python or Flask in the title. To accomplish this, we will create two contains expressions, then combine them using Python's bitwise OR operator, which is a pipe | character, unlike a lot of other languages that use a double pipe || character:

```
Entry.query.filter(Entry.title.contains('Python') |
Entry.title.contains('Flask'))
```

Using bitwise operators, we can come up with some pretty complex expressions. Try to figure out what the following example is asking for:

```
Entry.query.filter(
    (Entry.title.contains('Python') |
Entry.title.contains('Flask')) &
```

```
    (Entry.created_timestamp > (datetime.date.today() -
datetime.timedelta(days=30)))
    )
```

As you probably guessed, this query returns all entries where the title contains either `Python` or `Flask`, and that were created within the last 30 days. We are using Python's bitwise `OR` and `AND` operators to combine the sub-expressions. For any query you produce, you can view the generated SQL by printing the query as follows:

```
In []: query = Entry.query.filter(
    (Entry.title.contains('Python') | Entry.title.contains('Flask'))
&
    (Entry.created_timestamp > (datetime.date.today() -
datetime.timedelta(days=30)))
)
In []: print str(query)
```

```
SELECT entry.id AS entry_id, ...
FROM entry
WHERE (
    (entry.title LIKE '%%' || :title_1 || '%%') OR (entry.title LIKE
'%%' || :title_2 || '%%')
) AND entry.created_timestamp > :created_timestamp_1
```

# Negation

There is one more piece to discuss, which is **negation**. If we wanted to get a list of all blog entries that did not contain `Python` or `Flask` in the title, how would we do that? SQLAlchemy provides two ways to create these types of expressions, using either Python's unary negation operator (~) or by calling `db.not_()`. This is how you would construct this query with SQLAlchemy:

Using unary negation:

```
In []: Entry.query.filter(~(Entry.title.contains('Python') |
Entry.title.contains('Flask')))
```

Using `db.not_()`:

```
In []: Entry.query.filter(db.not_(Entry.title.contains('Python') |
Entry.title.contains('Flask')))
```

# Operator precedence

Not all operations are considered equal to the Python interpreter. This is like in math class, where we learned that expressions such as *2 + 3 \* 4* are equal to *14* and not *20*, because the multiplication operation occurs first. In Python, bitwise operators all have a higher precedence than things such as equality tests, so this means that, when you are building your query expression, you have to pay attention to the parentheses. Let's look at some example Python expressions and see the corresponding query:

| Expression | Result |
|---|---|
| (Entry.title == 'Python' \| Entry.title == 'Flask') | Wrong! SQLAlchemy throws an error because the first thing to be evaluated is actually the 'Python' \| Entry.title! |
| (Entry.title == 'Python') \| (Entry.title == 'Flask') | Right. Returns entries where the title is either "Python" or "Flask". |
| ~Entry.title == 'Python' | Wrong! SQLAlchemy will turn this into a valid SQL query, but the results will not be meaningful. |
| ~(Entry.title == 'Python') | Right. Returns entries where the title is not equal to "Python". |

If you find yourself struggling with operator precedence, it's a safe bet to put parentheses around any comparison that uses ==, !=, <, <=, >, and >=.

# Building a tagging system

Tags are a lightweight taxonomy system that is perfect for blogs. Tags allow you to apply multiple categories to a blog post and allow multiple posts to be related to one another outside their category. On my own blog I use tags to organize the posts, so that people interested in reading my posts about Flask need only look under the "Flask" tag and find all the relevant posts. As per the spec that we discussed in *Chapter 1, Creating Your First Flask Application*, each blog entry can have as few or as many tags as you want, so a post about Flask might be tagged with both Flask and Python. Similarly, each tag (for example, Python) can have multiple entries associated with it. In database parlance, this is called a many-to-many relationship.

In order to model this, we must first create a model to store tags. This model will store the names of tags we use, so after we've added a few tags the table might look something like the following one:

| id | tag |
|----|-----|
| 1 | Python |
| 2 | Flask |
| 3 | Django |
| 4 | random-thoughts |

Let's open `models.py` and add a definition for the `Tag` model. Add the following class at the end of the file, below the `Entry` class:

```
class Tag(db.Model):
    id = db.Column(db.Integer, primary_key=True)
    name = db.Column(db.String(64))
    slug = db.Column(db.String(64), unique=True)

    def __init__(self, *args, **kwargs):
        super(Tag, self).__init__(*args, **kwargs)
        self.slug = slugify(self.name)

    def __repr__(self):
        return '<Tag %s>' % self.name
```

You've seen all of this before. We've added a primary key, which will be managed by the database, and a single column to store the name of the tag. The `name` column is marked as unique, so each tag will only be represented by a single row in this table, regardless of how many blog entries it appears on.

Now that we have models for both blog entries and tags, we need a third model to store the relationships between the two. When we wish to signify that a blog entry is tagged with a particular tag, we will store a reference in this table. The following is a diagram of what is happening at the database table level:

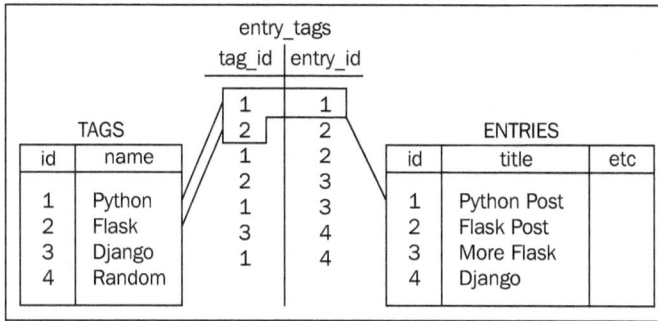

Since we will never be accessing this intermediary table directly (SQLAlchemy will handle it for us transparently), we will not create a model for it but will simply specify a table to store the mapping. Open `models.py` and add the following highlighted code:

```
import datetime, re

from app import db

def slugify(s):
    return re.sub('[^\w]+', '-', s).lower()

entry_tags = db.Table('entry_tags',
    db.Column('tag_id', db.Integer, db.ForeignKey('tag.id')),
    db.Column('entry_id', db.Integer, db.ForeignKey('entry.id'))
)

class Entry(db.Model):
    id = db.Column(db.Integer, primary_key=True)
    title = db.Column(db.String(100))
    slug = db.Column(db.String(100), unique=True)
    body = db.Column(db.Text)
    created_timestamp = db.Column(db.DateTime,
default=datetime.datetime.now)
    modified_timestamp = db.Column(
        db.DateTime,
        default=datetime.datetime.now,
        onupdate=datetime.datetime.now)

    tags = db.relationship('Tag', secondary=entry_tags,
        backref=db.backref('entries', lazy='dynamic'))

    def __init__(self, *args, **kwargs):
```

```
            super(Entry, self).__init__(*args, **kwargs)
            self.generate_slug()

        def generate_slug(self):
            self.slug = ''
            if self.title:
                self.slug = slugify(self.title)

        def __repr__(self):
            return '<Entry %s>' % self.title

    class Tag(db.Model):
        id = db.Column(db.Integer, primary_key=True)
        name = db.Column(db.String(64))
        slug = db.Column(db.String(64), unique=True)

        def __init__(self, *args, **kwargs):
            super(Tag, self).__init__(*args, **kwargs)
            self.slug = slugify(self.name)

        def __repr__(self):
            return '<Tag %s>' % self.name
```

By creating the `entry_tags` table, we have established a link between the `Entry` and `Tag` models. SQLAlchemy provides a high-level API for working with this relationship, the aptly-named `db.relationship` function. This function creates a new property on the `Entry` model that allows us to easily read and write the tags for a given blog entry. There is a lot going on in these two lines of code so let's take a closer look:

```
    tags = db.relationship('Tag', secondary=entry_tags,
        backref=db.backref('entries', lazy='dynamic'))
```

We are setting the tags attribute of the `Entry` class equal to the return value of the `db.relationship` function. The first two arguments, `'Tag'` and `secondary=entry_tags`, instruct SQLAlchemy that we are going to be querying the `Tag` model via the `entry_tags` table. The third argument creates a back-reference, allowing us to go from the `Tag` model back to the associated list of blog entries. By specifying `lazy='dynamic'`, we instruct SQLAlchemy that, instead of it loading all the associated entries for us, we want a Query object instead.

# Adding and removing tags from entries

Let's use the IPython shell to see how this works. Close your current shell and re-run the `scripts/create_db.py` script. This step is necessary since we added two new tables. Now re-open IPython:

```
(blog) $ python scripts/create_db.py
(blog) $ ipython
In []: from models import *
In []: Tag.query.all()
Out[]: []
```

There are currently no tags in the database, so let's create a couple of them:

```
In []: python = Tag(name='python')
In []: flask = Tag(name='flask')
In []: db.session.add_all([python, flask])
In []: db.session.commit()
```

Now let's load up some example entries. In my database there are four:

```
In []: Entry.query.all()
Out[]:
[<Entry Python entry>,
 <Entry Flask entry>,
 <Entry More flask>,
 <Entry Django entry>]
In []: python_entry, flask_entry, more_flask, django_entry = _
```

> In IPython, you can use an underscore (_) to reference the return-value of the previous line.

To add tags to an entry, simply assign them to the entry's `tags` attribute. It's that easy!

```
In []: python_entry.tags = [python]
In []: flask_entry.tags = [python, flask]
In []: db.session.commit()
```

We can work with an entry's list of tags just like a normal Python list, so the usual `.append()` and `.remove()` methods will also work:

```
In []: kittens = Tag(name='kittens')
In []: python_entry.tags.append(kittens)
In []: db.session.commit()
In []: python_entry.tags
Out[]: [<Tag python>, <Tag kittens>]
In []: python_entry.tags.remove(kittens)
In []: db.session.commit()
In []: python_entry.tags
Out[]: [<Tag python>]
```

# Using backrefs

When we created the `tags` attribute on the `Entry` model, you will recall we passed in a `backref` argument. Let's use IPython to see how the back-reference is used.

```
In []: python  # The python variable is just a tag.
Out[]: <Tag python>
In []: python.entries
Out[]: <sqlalchemy.orm.dynamic.AppenderBaseQuery at 0x332ff90>
In []: python.entries.all()
Out[]: [<Entry Flask entry>, <Entry Python entry>]
```

Unlike the `Entry.tags` reference, the back-reference is specified as `lazy='dynamic'`. This means that, unlike `entry.tags`, which gives us a list of tags, we will not receive a list of entries every time we access `tag.entries`. Why is this? Typically, when the result-set is larger than a few items, it is more useful to treat the `backref` argument as a query, which can be filtered, ordered, and so on. For example, what if we wanted to show the latest entry tagged with `python`?

```
In []: python.entries.order_by(Entry.created_timestamp.desc()).first()
Out[]: <Entry Flask entry>
```

> The SQLAlchemy documentation contains an excellent overview of the various values that you can use for the lazy argument. You can find them online at `http://docs.sqlalchemy.org/en/rel_0_9/orm/relationships.html#sqlalchemy.orm.relationship.params.lazy`

# Making changes to the schema

The final topic we will discuss in this chapter is how to make modifications to an existing Model definition. From the project specification, we know we would like to be able to save drafts of our blog entries. Right now we don't have any way to tell whether an entry is a draft or not, so we will need to add a column that lets us store the status of our entry. Unfortunately, while db.create_all() works perfectly for creating tables, it will not automatically modify an existing table; to do this we need to use migrations.

# Adding Flask-Migrate to our project

We will use Flask-Migrate to help us automatically update our database whenever we change the schema. In the blog virtualenv, install Flask-Migrate using pip:

```
(blog) $ pip install flask-migrate
```

> The author of SQLAlchemy has a project called alembic; Flask-Migrate makes use of this and integrates it with Flask directly, making things easier.

Next we will add a Migrate helper to our app. We will also create a script manager for our app. The script manager allows us to execute special commands within the context of our app, directly from the command-line. We will be using the script manager to execute the migrate command. Open app.py and make the following additions:

```
from flask import Flask
from flask.ext.migrate import Migrate, MigrateCommand
from flask.ext.script import Manager
from flask.ext.sqlalchemy import SQLAlchemy

from config import Configuration

app = Flask(__name__)
app.config.from_object(Configuration)
db = SQLAlchemy(app)
migrate = Migrate(app, db)

manager = Manager(app)
manager.add_command('db', MigrateCommand)
```

In order to use the manager, we will add a new file named `manage.py` along with `app.py`. Add the following code to `manage.py`:

```
from app import manager
from main import *

if __name__ == '__main__':
    manager.run()
```

This looks very similar to `main.py`, the key difference being, instead of calling `app.run()`, we are calling `manager.run()`.

> Django has a similar, although auto-generated, `manage.py` file that serves a similar function.

# Creating the initial migration

Before we can start changing our schema, we need to create a record of its current state. To do this, run the following commands from inside your blog's app directory. The first command will create a migrations directory inside the `app` folder that will track the changes we make to our schema. The second command `db migrate` will create a snapshot of our current schema so that future changes can be compared to it.

```
(blog) $ python manage.py db init

  Creating directory /home/charles/projects/blog/app/migrations ... done

  ...
(blog) $ python manage.py db migrate
INFO    [alembic.migration] Context impl SQLiteImpl.
INFO    [alembic.migration] Will assume non-transactional DDL.

  Generating /home/charles/projects/blog/app/migrations/
versions/535133f91f00_.py ... done
```

Finally, we will run `db upgrade` to run the migration that will indicate to the migration system that everything is up-to-date:

```
(blog) $ python manage.py db upgrade
INFO    [alembic.migration] Context impl SQLiteImpl.
INFO    [alembic.migration] Will assume non-transactional DDL.
INFO    [alembic.migration] Running upgrade None -> 535133f91f00, empty
message
```

# Adding a status column

Now that we have a snapshot of our current schema, we can start making changes. We will be adding a new column, named status, that will store an integer value corresponding to a particular status. Although there are only two statuses at the moment (PUBLIC and DRAFT), using an integer instead of a Boolean gives us the option to easily add more statuses in the future. Open models.py and make the following additions to the Entry model:

```python
class Entry(db.Model):
    STATUS_PUBLIC = 0
    STATUS_DRAFT = 1

    id = db.Column(db.Integer, primary_key=True)
    title = db.Column(db.String(100))
    slug = db.Column(db.String(100), unique=True)
    body = db.Column(db.Text)
    status = db.Column(db.SmallInteger, default=STATUS_PUBLIC)
    created_timestamp = db.Column(db.DateTime,
default=datetime.datetime.now)
    . . .
```

From the command-line, we will once again be running db migrate to generate the migration script. You can see from the command's output that it found our new column!

```
(blog) $ python manage.py db migrate
INFO   [alembic.migration] Context impl SQLiteImpl.
INFO   [alembic.migration] Will assume non-transactional DDL.
INFO   [alembic.autogenerate.compare] Detected added column 'entry.status'
  Generating /home/charles/projects/blog/app/migrations/
versions/2c8e81936cad_.py ... done
```

Because we have blog entries in the database, we need to make a small modification to the auto-generated migration to ensure the statuses for the existing entries are initialized to the proper value. To do this, open up the migration file (mine is migrations/versions/2c8e81936cad_.py) and change the following line:

```python
op.add_column('entry', sa.Column('status', sa.SmallInteger(),
nullable=True))
```

Replacing `nullable=True` with `server_default='0'` tells the migration script to not set the column to null by default, but instead to use `0`.

```
op.add_column('entry', sa.Column('status', sa.SmallInteger(), server_
default='0'))
```

Finally, run `db upgrade` to run the migration and create the status column.

```
(blog) $ python manage.py db upgrade
INFO    [alembic.migration] Context impl SQLiteImpl.
INFO    [alembic.migration] Will assume non-transactional DDL.
INFO    [alembic.migration] Running upgrade 535133f91f00 -> 2c8e81936cad,
empty message
```

Congratulations, your `Entry` model now has a status field!

# Summary

By now you should be familiar with using SQLAlchemy to work with a relational database. We covered the benefits of using a relational database and an ORM, configured a Flask application to connect to a relational database, and created SQLAlchemy models. All this allowed us to create relationships between our data and perform queries. To top it off, we also used a migration tool to handle future database schema changes.

In *Chapter 3, Templates and Views* we will set aside the interactive interpreter and start creating views to display blog entries in the web browser. We will put all our SQLAlchemy knowledge to work by creating interesting lists of blog entries, as well as a simple search feature. We will build a set of templates to make the blogging site visually appealing, and learn how to use the Jinja2 templating language to eliminate repetitive HTML coding. It will be a fun chapter!

# 3
# Templates and Views

This chapter could alternatively be titled *The Flask Chapter*, because we will cover two of the most recognizable components of the framework: the Jinja2 template language, and the URL routing framework. Up to this point, we have been laying the foundation for the blog app, but we have barely scratched the surface of actual Flask development. In this chapter, we will dive into Flask and see our app finally start taking shape. We will turn our drab database models into dynamically rendered HTML pages, using templates. We will come up with a URL scheme that reflects the ways we wish to organize our blog entries. As we progress through the chapter, our blog app will start looking like a proper website.

In this chapter we shall:

- Learn how to render HTML templates using Jinja2
- Learn how to use loops, control structures, and the filters provided by the Jinja2 template language
- Use template inheritance to eliminate repetitive coding
- Create a clean URL scheme for our blog app and set up the routing from URLs to views
- Render lists of blog entries using Jinja2 templates
- Add full-text search to the site

# Introducing Jinja2

Jinja2 is a fast, flexible, and secure templating engine. It allows you to define your website in small blocks that are pieced together to form complete pages. On our blog, for instance, we will have blocks for the header, the sidebar, the footer, as well as templates, for rendering blog posts. This approach is **DRY (Don't Repeat Yourself)**, which means that the markup contained in each block should not be copied or pasted elsewhere. Since the HTML for each part of the site exists in only one place, making changes and fixing bugs is much easier. Jinja2 also allows you to embed display logic in the template. For instance, we may wish to display a log out button to users who are logged in, but display a log in form to users browsing anonymously. As you will see, it is very easy to accomplish these types of things with a bit of template logic.

From the beginning, Flask was built with Jinja2 in mind, so working with templates in your Flask app is extremely easy. Since Jinja2 is a requirement of the Flask framework, it is already installed in our virtualenv, so we're able to get started immediately.

Create a new folder named `templates` in the blog project's `app` directory. Create a single file inside the template folder named `homepage.html` and add the following HTML code:

```
<!doctype html>
<html>
  <head>
    <title>Blog</title>
  </head>
  <body>
    <h1>Welcome to my blog</h1>
  </body>
</html>
```

Now open `views.py` in the blog project's `app` directory. We are going to modify our `homepage` view to render the new `homepage.html` template. To do this, we will use Flask's `render_template()` function, passing in the name of our template as the first argument. Rendering a template is an extremely common action, so Flask makes this part as easy as possible:

```
from flask import render_template

from app import app

@app.route('/')
```

```
def homepage():
    return render_template('homepage.html')
```

Using the `manage.py` helper that we created in the previous chapter, start the development server and navigate to `http://127.0.0.1:5000/` to view the rendered template, as shown in the following screenshot:

```
(blog) $ python manage.py runserver
* Running on http://127.0.0.1:5000/
* Restarting with reloader
```

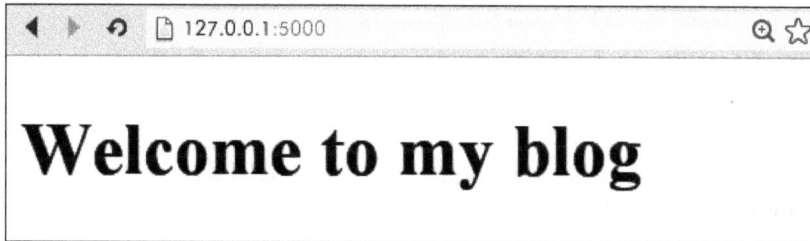

# Basic template operations

The previous example may not seem very impressive, since we are doing little more than serving a plain HTML document. To make things interesting, we need to give our templates **context**. Let's modify our homepage to display a simple greeting to illustrate the point. Open `views.py` and make the following modifications:

```
from flask import render_template, request

from app import app

@app.route('/')
def homepage():
    name = request.args.get('name')
    if not name:
        name = '<unknown>'
    return render_template('homepage.html', name=name)
```

In the view code, we are passing `name` into the template context. The next step is to do something with that `name` inside the actual template. In this example, we will simply print the value of `name`. Open `homepage.html` and make the following addition:

```
<!doctype html>
<html>
  <head>
    <title>Blog</title>
  </head>
  <body>
    <h1>Welcome to my blog</h1>
    <p>Your name is {{ name }}.</p>
  </body>
</html>
```

Start the development server and navigate to the root URL. You should see something like the following image:

Any keyword arguments passed to the `render_template` function are available in the template context. In the template language of Jinja2, double brackets are analogous to a `print` statement. We use the `{{ name }}` operation to output the value of `name`, which is set to `<unknown>`.

> The security-minded reader may have noticed that, when we viewed our template in the browser, the brackets were escaped. Ordinarily, brackets are treated by the browser as HTML markup, but, as you can see, Jinja2 has escaped the brackets automatically, replacing them with `&lt;` and `&gt;`.

Try navigating to a URL such as `http://127.0.0.1:5000/?name=Charlie`.
Whatever value you specify will appear, rendered for us automatically by Jinja2, as
seen in the following image

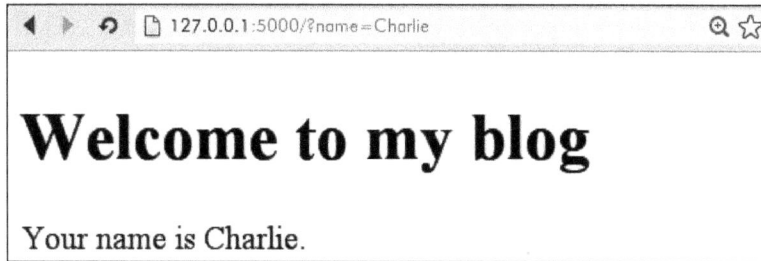

Suppose someone malicious visits your site and wants to cause some trouble.
Noticing that values from the query-string are passed directly into the template, this
person decides to have some fun by attempting to inject a script tag. Thankfully for
us, Jinja2 automatically escapes values before inserting them into the rendered page.

# Loops, control structures, and template programming

Jinja2 supports a miniature programming language that can be used to perform
operations on data within the context. If all we could do was print values to the
context, there honestly wouldn't be too much to be excited about. Things get
interesting when we combine contextual data with things such as loops and
control structures.

Let's modify our homepage view once more. This time we will accept a number, in addition to a name, from `request.args` and display all the even numbers between 0 and that number. The neat part is that we will do almost all of this in the template. Make the following changes to `views.py`:

```python
from flask import render_template, request

from app import app

@app.route('/')
def homepage():
    name = request.args.get('name')
    number = request.args.get('number')
    return render_template('homepage.html', name=name, number=number)
```

Now open the `hompage.html` template and add the following code. If it seems odd, don't worry. We will go through it line by line.

```html
<!doctype html>
<html>
  <head>
    <title>Blog</title>
  </head>
  <body>
    <h1>Welcome to my blog</h1>
    {% if number %}
      <p>Your number is {{ number|int }}</p>
      <ul>
        {% for i in range(number|int) %}
          {% if i is divisibleby 2 %}
            <li>{{ i }}</li>
          {% endif %}
        {% endfor %}
      </ul>
    {% else %}
      <p>No number specified.</p>
    {% endif %}

    <p>Your name is {{ name|default('<unknown>', True) }}.</p>
  </body>
</html>
```

Start a runserver and experiment by passing some values in using the query-string. Also, take note of what happens when you pass a non-numeric value or a negative value.

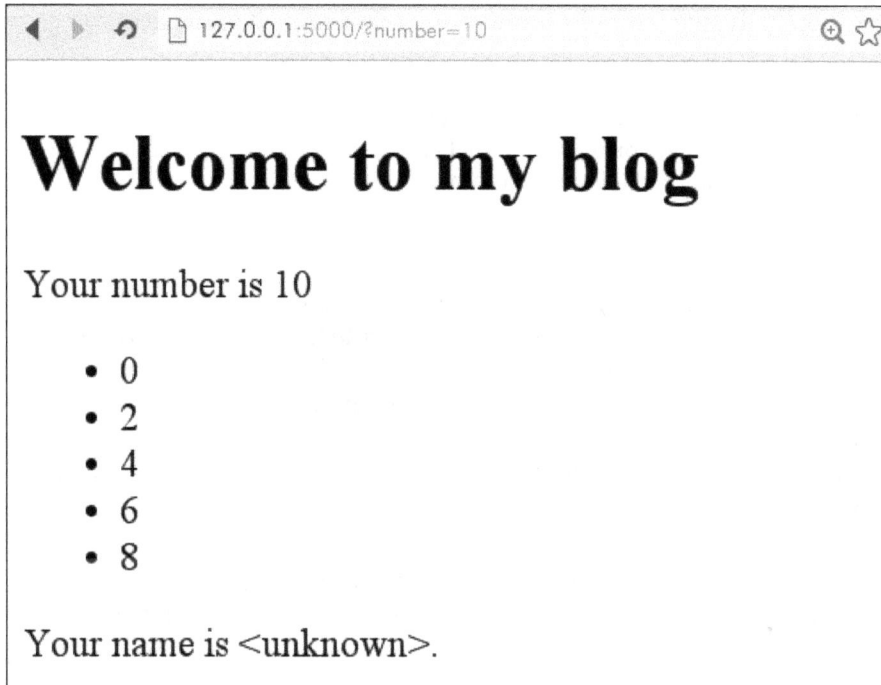

Let's go through our new template code line by line, starting with the {% if number %} statement. Unlike the print tags that use double curly brackets, logical tags use {% and %}. We are simply checking whether or not a number was passed into the context. If the number is None or an empty string, this test will fail, just as it would in Python.

The next line prints the integer representation of our number and uses a new syntax, |int. The pipe symbol (|) is used in Jinja2 to indicate a call to a filter. A **filter** performs some type of operation on the value to the left side of the pipe symbol, and returns a new value. In this case, we are using the built-in int filter that converts a string to an integer, defaulting to 0 when a number cannot be determined. There are many filters built into Jinja2; we will discuss them later in the chapter.

The {% for %} statement is used to create a *for* loop and looks remarkably close to Python. We are using the Jinja2 range helper to generate a series of numbers with [0, number). Note that we are again piping the number context value through the int filter in the call to range. Also note that we are assigning a value to a new context variable i. Inside the loop body, we can use i just like any other context variable.

> Of course, just like in regular Python, we can also use an {% else %} statement on a for-loop that can be used to run some code in the eventuality that there is nothing for the loop to do.

Now that we are looping through the numbers, we need to check whether i is even, and if so, print it. Jinja2 provides several ways we could do this, but I have chosen to show the use of a Jinja2 feature called **tests**. Like filters and control structures, Jinja2 also comes with a number of useful tools for testing the attributes of a context value. Tests are used in conjunction with {% if %} statements and are denoted by the use of the keyword is. So we have {% if i is divisibleby 2 %}, which is very easy to read. If the if statement evaluates to True then we will print the value of i using double braces: {{ i }}.

> Jinja2 provides a number of useful tests; to learn more check the project documentation at http://jinja.pocoo.org/docs/templates/#tests.

Since Jinja2 is not aware of significant whitespace, we need to explicitly close all our logical tags. That is why you see an {% endif %} tag, signifying the closing of the divisibleby 2 check, and an {% endfor %}, signifying the closing of the for i in range loop. After the for loop, we are now in the outermost if statement, which tests whether a number was passed into the context. In the event no number is present, we want to print a message to the user so, before calling {% endif %}, we will use an {% else %} tag to display this message.

Finally, we have changed the line that prints a greeting to the user to read {{ name|default('<unknown>', True) }}. In the view code, we removed the logic that set it to a default value of <unknown>. Instead, we have moved that logic into the template. Here we see the default filter (denoted by the | character) but, unlike int, we are passing multiple arguments. In Jinja2, a filter can take multiple arguments. By convention, the first argument appears to the left of the pipe symbol, since filters frequently operate on single values. In the event there are multiple arguments, these are specified in parentheses *after* the filter name. In the case of the default filter, we have specified the value to use in the event no name is specified.

# Jinja2 built-in filters

In the previous example, we saw how to use the `int` filter to coerce a context value to an integer. Along with `int`, Jinja2 provides a large array of useful built-in filters. For reasons of space (the list is very long), I will only include the most frequently-used filters from my experience, but the entire list can be found online at `http://jinja.pocoo.org/docs/templates/#list-of-builtin-filters`.

> In the following examples, the first argument in the argument list would appear to the left-hand side of the pipe symbol. So, even though I have written `abs (number)`, the filter used would be `number|abs`. When the filter accepts more than one parameter, the remaining parameters appear in parentheses after the filter name.

| Filter and parameter(s) | Description and return value |
| --- | --- |
| abs(number) | Returns the absolute value of the number. |
| default(value, default_value='', boolean=False) | In the event `value` is undefined (i.e., the name does not exist in the context) use the provided `default_value` instead. In the event you simply want to test whether `value` evaluates to a boolean `True` (i.e., not an empty string, the number zero, None, and so on.), then pass `True` as the third argument: <br><br>`{{ not_in_context|default:"The value was not in the context" }}`<br><br>`{{ ''|default('An empty string.', True) }}` |
| dictsort(value, case_sensitive=False, by='key') | Sorts a dictionary by key, yielding `(key, value)` pairs. You can also, however, sort by value.<br><br>`<p>Alphabetically by name.</p>`<br>`{% for name, age in people|dictsort %}`<br>`    {{ name }} is {{ age }}`<br>`years old.`<br>`{% endfor %}`<br><br>`<p>Youngest to oldest.</p>`<br>`{% for name, age in people|dictsort(by='value') %}`<br>`    {{ name }} is {{ age }}`<br>`years old.`<br>`{% endfor %}` |

| Filter and parameter(s) | Description and return value |
|---|---|
| int(value, default=0) | Converts `value` to an integer. In the event the value cannot be converted, use the specified default. |
| length(object) | Returns the number of items in the collection. |
| reverse(sequence) | Reverses the sequence. |
| safe(value) | Outputs the value unescaped. This filter is useful when you have trusted HTML that you wish to print. For instance, if `value = "<b>"`:<br><br>`{{ value }} --> outputs`<br>`&lt;b&gt;`<br><br>`{{ value|safe }} --> outputs`<br>`<b>` |
| sort(value, reverse=False, case_sensitive=False, attribute=None) | Sorts an iterable value. If `reverse` is specified, the items will be sorted in reverse order. If the `attribute` parameter is used, that attribute will be treated as the value to sort by. |
| striptags(value) | Removes any HTML tags, useful for cleaning up and outputting untrusted user input. |
| truncate(value, length=255, killwords=False, end='...') | Returns a truncated copy of the string. The length parameter specifies how many characters to keep. If `killwords` is `False`, then a word may be chopped in half; if `True` then Jinja2 will truncate at the previous word boundary. In the event the value exceeds the length and needs to be truncated, the value in `end` will be appended automatically. |
| urlize(value, trim_url_limit=None, nofollow=False, target=None) | Converts URLs in plain text into clickable links. |

Filters can be chained together, so `{{ number|int|abs }}` would first convert the number variable to an integer, then return its absolute value.

# Creating a base template for the blog

Jinja2's inheritance and include features make it is very easy to define a base template that serves as the architectural foundation for each page on your site. The base template contains basic structural things that should never change, such as the `<html>`, `<head>`, and `<body>` tags, as well as the basic structure of the body. It can also be used to include style sheets or scripts that will be served on every page. Most importantly, the base template is responsible for defining overrideable blocks, into which we will place page-specific content such as the page title and body content.

In order to get up-and-running quickly, we will be using Twitter's Bootstrap library (version 3). This will allow us to focus on how templates are structured and have a decent-looking site with minimal extra work. You are, of course, welcome to use your own CSS if you prefer, but the example code will use bootstrap-specific constructs.

Create a new file in the `templates` directory named `base.html`, and add the following content:

```html
<!DOCTYPE html>
<html lang="en">
  <head>
    <meta charset="utf-8">
    <title>{% block title %}{% endblock %} | My Blog</title>
    <link rel="stylesheet"
href="//netdna.bootstrapcdn.com/bootstrap/3.1.0/css/bootstrap.min.
css">
    <style type="text/css">
      body { padding-top: 60px; }
    </style>
    {% block extra_styles %}{% endblock %}

    <script src=
"https://code.jquery.com/jquery-1.10.2.min.js"></script>
    <script
src="//netdna.bootstrapcdn.com/bootstrap/3.1.0/js/
bootstrap.min.js"></script>
    {% block extra_scripts %}{% endblock %}
  </head>

  <body class="{% block body_class %}{% endblock %}">
    <div class="navbar navbar-inverse navbar-fixed-top"
role="navigation">
      <div class="container">
        <div class="navbar-header">
```

```
              <button type="button" class="navbar-toggle"
data-toggle="collapse" data-target=".navbar-collapse">
                    <span class="sr-only">Toggle navigation</span>
                    <span class="icon-bar"></span>
                    <span class="icon-bar"></span>
                    <span class="icon-bar"></span>
              </button>
              <a class="navbar-brand" href="#">{% block branding %}My
Blog{% endblock %}</a>
          </div>
          <div class="collapse navbar-collapse">
            <ul class="nav navbar-nav">
              <li><a href="/">Home</a></li>
              {% block extra_nav %}{% endblock %}
            </ul>
          </div>
        </div>
      </div>
      <div class="container">
        <div class="row">
          <div class="col-md-9">
            <h1>{% block content_title %}{% endblock %}</h1>
            {% block content %}
            {% endblock %}
          </div>
          <div class="col-md-3">
            {% block sidebar %}
            <ul class="well nav nav-stacked">
              <li><a href="#">Sidebar item</a></li>
            </ul>
            {% endblock %}
          </div>
        </div>
        <div class="row">
          <hr />
          <footer>
            <p>&copy; your name</p>
          </footer>
        </div>
      </div>
    </body>
</html>
```

Interspersed alongside the markup is a new Jinja2 tag, `block`. The `block` tags are used to indicate overrideable areas of the page.

You may have noticed that we are serving jQuery and Bootstrap from publicly-available URLs. In the next chapter, we will discuss how to serve static files that are stored locally on disk. Now we can modify our homepage template and take advantage of the new base template. We can do this by extending the base template and overriding certain blocks. This works very similar to class inheritance that you find in most languages. As long as the sections of the inherited page are split up into blocks nicely, we can override only the bits we need to change. Let's open `homepage.html` and replace some of the current contents with the following:

```
{% extends "base.html" %}

{% block content_title %}Welcome to my blog{% endblock %}

{% block content %}
  {% if number %}
    <p>Your number is {{ number|int }}</p>
    <ul>
      {% for i in range(number|int) %}
        {% if i is divisibleby 2 %}
          <li>{{ i }}</li>
        {% endif %}
      {% endfor %}
    </ul>
  {% else %}
    <p>No number specified.</p>
  {% endif %}

  <p>Your name is {{ name|default('<unknown>', True) }}.</p>
{% endblock %}
```

By extending the original page, we have removed all the HTML boilerplate and a lot of complexity, focusing only on what makes this page, our homepage view, unique. Start up the server and navigate to `http://127.0.0.1:5000/`, you will see that our homepage has been transformed.

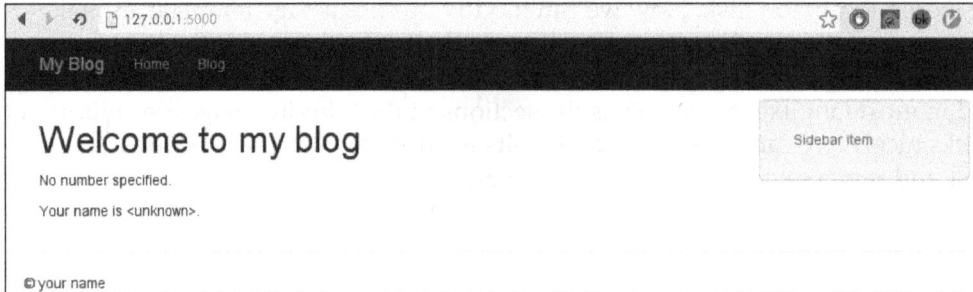

Congratulations! You have now learned some of the most commonly-used features of Jinja2. There are many more advanced features that we have not covered in the interests of time, and I would recommend reading the project's documentation to see the full range of possibilities with Jinja2. The documentation can be found at `http://jinja.pocoo.org/docs/`.

We still need to build templates to display our blog entries. Before continuing to build out templates, though, we first must create some view functions that will generate the lists of blog entries. We will then pass the entries into the context, just as we did with the homepage.

# Creating a URL scheme

URLs are for people, therefore they should be easy to remember. A good URL scheme is easy to remember when it accurately reflects the implicit structure of the website. Our goal is to create a URL scheme that makes it easy for the visitors on our site to find blog entries on topics that interest them.

Referring back to the spec we created in *Chapter 1, Creating Your First Flask Application*, we know that we want our blog entries to be organized by tag and by date. Entries organized by tag and date will necessarily be a subset of the collection of all entries, so that gives us a structure like this:

| URL | Purpose |
| --- | --- |
| /entries/ | This displays all of our blog entries, ordered most-recent first |
| /entries/tags/ | This contains all the tags used to organize our blog entries |
| /entries/tags/python/ | This contains all the entries tagged with python |
| /entries/learning-the-flask-framework/ | This is a detail page showing the body content for a blog entry titled *Learning the Flask Framework* |

Since a single blog entry may be associated with multiple tags, how do we decide what to use as its canonical URL? If I wrote a blog entry titled *Learning the Flask framework*, I could conceivably nest it under /entries/, /entries/tags/python/, /entries/tags/flask/, and so on. That would violate one of the rules about good URLs, which is that a unique resource should have one, and only one, URL. For that reason, I am going to advocate putting individual blog entries at the top of the hierarchy:

/entries/learning-the-flask-framework/

News sites and blogs with a large amount of time-sensitive content will typically nest individual pieces of content using the publication date. This prevents collisions when two articles might share the same title, but have been written at different times. When a lot of content is produced each day, this scheme often makes more sense:

/entries/2014/jan/18/learning-the-flask-framework/

Although we will not be covering this type of URL scheme in this chapter, the code can be found online at http://www.packtpub.com/support.

# Defining the URL routes

Let's convert the structure described previously into some URL routes that Flask will understand. Create a new directory named `entries` in the blog project's `app` directory. Inside the `entries` directory, create two files, `__init__.py` and `blueprint.py` as follows:

```
(blog) $ mkdir entries
(blog) $ touch entries/{__init__,blueprint}.py
```

**Blueprints** provide a nice API for encapsulating a group of related routes and templates. In smaller applications, typically everything gets registered on the app object (that is, `app.route`). When an application has distinct components, as ours does, blueprints can be used to separate the various moving parts. Since the `/entries/` URL is going to be devoted entirely to our blog entries, we will create a blueprint and then define views to handle the routes that we described previously. Open `blueprint.py` and add the following code:

```python
from flask import Blueprint

from models import Entry, Tag

entries = Blueprint('entries', __name__,
template_folder='templates')

@entries.route('/')
def index():
    return 'Entries index'

@entries.route('/tags/')
def tag_index():
    pass

@entries.route('/tags/<slug>/')
def tag_detail(slug):
    pass

@entries.route('/<slug>/')
def detail(slug):
    pass
```

These URL routes are placeholders that we will fill in shortly, but I wanted to show you how clean and simple it is to translate a set of URL patterns into a set of routes and views.

In order to access these new views, we need to register our blueprint with our main Flask `app` object. We will also instruct our app that we want our entries' URLs to live at the prefix `/entries`. Open `main.py` and make the following additions:

```
from app import app, db
import models
import views

from entries.blueprint import entries
app.register_blueprint(entries, url_prefix='/entries')

if __name__ == '__main__':
    app.run()
```

If you want to test it out, start the debug server (`python manage.py runserver`) and navigate to `http://127.0.0.1:5000/entries/`. You should see the following message:

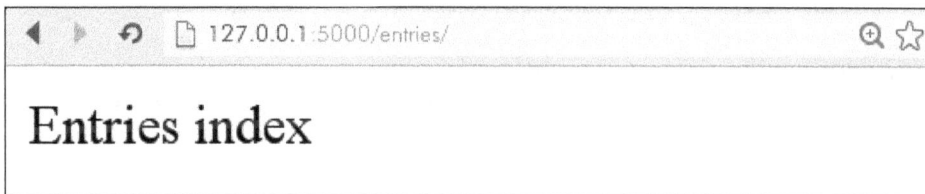

## Building the index view

The `index` view is the top-most URL in our `/entries/` hierarchy, and as such will contain all the entries. After a time we might have tens or even hundreds of blog entries, so we will want to paginate this list so as not to overwhelm our visitors (or our server!). Because we will frequently be displaying lists of objects, let's create a helpers module that will make it easy to display paginated lists of objects. In the `app` directory, create a new module named `helpers.py` and add the following code:

```
from flask import render_template, request

def object_list(template_name, query, paginate_by=20, **context):
    page = request.args.get('page')
    if page and page.isdigit():
        page = int(page)
    else:
        page = 1
```

```
        object_list = query.paginate(page, paginate_by)
        return render_template(template_name, object_list=object_list,
    **context)
```

Now, we will open `entries/blueprint.py` and modify the `index` view to return a paginated list of entries:

```
from flask import Blueprint

from helpers import object_list
from models import Entry, Tag

entries = Blueprint('entries', __name__,
template_folder='templates')

@entries.route('/')
def index():
    entries = Entry.query.order_by(Entry.created_timestamp.desc())
    return object_list('entries/index.html', entries)
```

We are importing the `object_list` helper function and passing it the name of a template and the query representing the entries we wish to display. As we build out the rest of these views, you will see how little helper functions such as `object_list` make Flask development quite easy.

The final piece is the `entries/index.html` template. In the `entries` directory, create a directory named `templates`, and a sub-directory named `entries`. Create `index.html` such that the full path from the `app` directory is `entries/templates/entries/index.html` and add the following code:

```
{% extends "base.html" %}

{% block title %}Entries{% endblock %}

{% block content_title %}Entries{% endblock %}

{% block content %}
  {% include "includes/list.html" %}
{% endblock %}
```

This template is very minimal, all the work will happen in `includes/list.html`. The `{% include %}` tag is new, and is useful for reusable template fragments. Create the file `includes/list.html` and add the following code:

```
{% for entry in object_list.items %}
```

```
<p><a href="{{ url_for('entries.detail', slug=entry.slug) }}">{{
entry.title }}</a></p>
{% endfor %}
```

The `url_for` function is extremely useful. `url_for()` allows us to provide the name of a view function or any arguments, and then generates the URL. Since the URL we wish to reference is the `detail` view of the entries blueprint, the name of the view is `entries.detail`. The detail view accepts a single argument, the slug of the entry's title.

Before building out the detail view, re-open the base template and add a link to the entries in the navigation section:

```
<ul class="nav navbar-nav">
  <li><a href="{{ url_for('homepage') }}">Home</a></li>
  <li><a href="{{ url_for('entries.index') }}">Blog</a></li>
  {% block extra_nav %}{% endblock %}
</ul>
```

The following screenshot shows the updated navigation header, along with a list of blog entries:

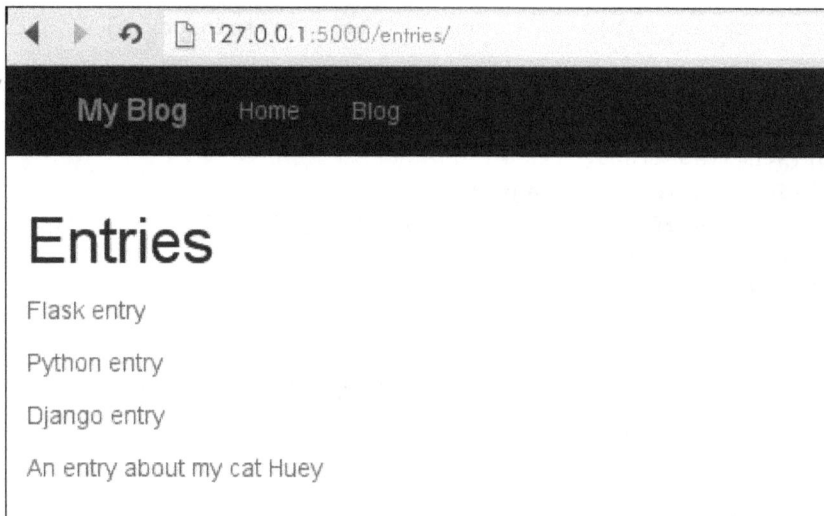

# Building the detail view

Let's create a simple view that will render the contents of a single blog entry. The slug of the entry will be passed in as a part of the URL. We will attempt to match that to an existing Entry, returning a 404 response if none matches. Update the following code to the detail view in the entries blueprint:

```
from flask import render_template
@entries.route('/<slug>/')
def detail(slug):
    entry = Entry.query.filter(Entry.slug == slug).first_or_404()
    return render_template('entries/detail.html', entry=entry)
```

Create a template in the entries template directory named detail.html and add the following code. We will display the title and body of the entry in the main content area, but in the sidebar we will display a list of tags and the date the entry was created:

```
{% extends "base.html" %}

{% block title %}{{ entry.title }}{% endblock %}

{% block content_title %}{{ entry.title }}{% endblock %}

{% block sidebar %}
  <ul class="well nav nav-list">
    <li><h4>Tags</h4></li>
    {% for tag in entry.tags %}
      <li><a href="{{ url_for('entries.tag_detail', slug=tag.slug)
}}">{{ tag.name }}</a></li>
    {% endfor %}
  </ul>

  <p>Published {{ entry.created_timestamp.strftime('%m/%d/%Y')
}}</p>
{% endblock %}

{% block content %}
  {{ entry.body }}
{% endblock %}
```

It should now be possible to view entries on the index page and follow the link to the details view. As you probably guessed, the next thing we need to tackle is the tag detail page.

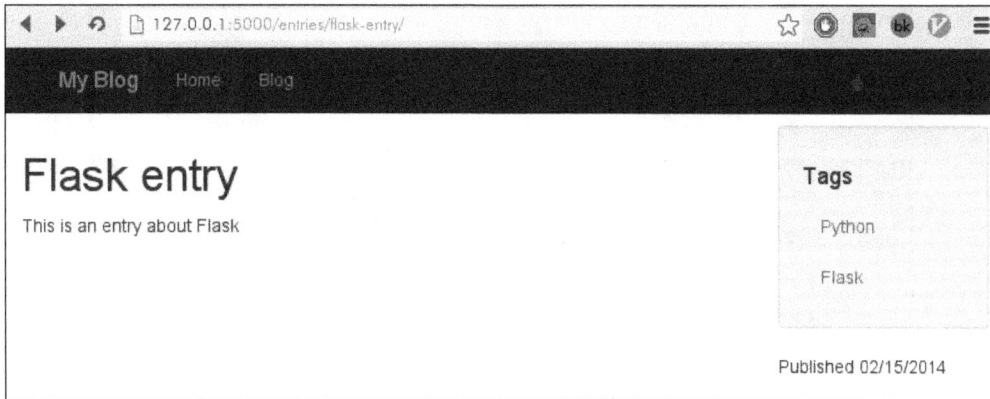

# Listing entries matching a given tag

Listing the entries that match a given tag will combine the logic from the two previous views. First we will need to look up the `Tag` using the `tag` slug provided in the URL, and then we will display an `object_list` of `Entry` objects that are tagged with the specified tag. In the `tag_detail` view, add the following code:

```python
@entries.route('/tags/<slug>/')
def tag_detail(slug):
    tag = Tag.query.filter(Tag.slug == slug).first_or_404()
    entries = tag.entries.order_by(Entry.created_timestamp.desc())
    return object_list('entries/tag_detail.html', entries,
tag=tag)
```

The `entries` query will get all the entries associated with the tag, then return them ordered most-recent first. We are also passing the tag into the context so we can display it in the template. Create the `tag_detail.html` template and add the following code. Since we are going to display a list of entries, we will re-use our `list.html` include:

```html
{% extends "base.html" %}

{% block title %}{{ tag.name }} entries{% endblock %}

{% block content_title %}{{ tag.name }} entries{% endblock %}

{% block content %}
  {% include "includes/list.html" %}
{% endblock %}
```

In the following screenshot, I have navigated to /entries/tags/python/. This page only contains entries that have been tagged with *Python*:

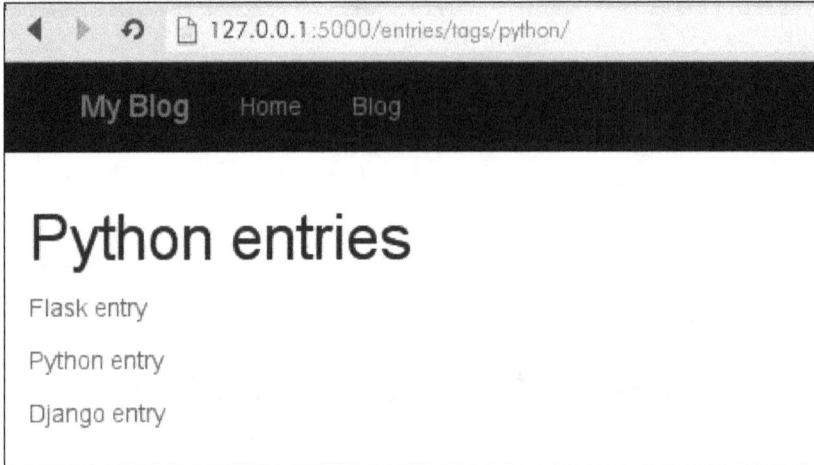

## Listing all the tags

The final missing piece is the view that will display a list of all the tags. This view will be very similar to the index entry, except that, instead of Entry objects, we will be querying the Tag model. Update the following code to the tag_index view:

```
@entries.route('/tags/')
def tag_index():
    tags = Tag.query.order_by(Tag.name)
    return object_list('entries/tag_index.html', tags)
```

In the template, we will display each tag as a link to the corresponding tag detail page. Create the file entries/tag_index.html and add the following code:

```
{% extends "base.html" %}

{% block title %}Tags{% endblock %}

{% block content_title %}Tags{% endblock %}

{% block content %}
  <ul>
    {% for tag in object_list.items %}
      <li><a href="{{ url_for('entries.tag_detail', slug=tag.slug)
}}">{{ tag.name }}</a></li>
```

```
    {% endfor %}
  </ul>
{% endblock %}
```

If you like, you can add a link to the tag list in the base template's navigation.

# Full-text search

In order to allow users to find posts containing certain words or phrases, we will add simple full-text search to the pages that contain lists of blog entries. To accomplish this, we will do some refactoring. We will be adding a search form to the sidebar of all pages containing lists of blog entries. While we could copy and paste the same code into both `entries/index.html` and `entries/tag_detail.html`, we will, instead, create another base template that contains the search widget. Create a new template named `entries/base_entries.html` and add the following code:

```
{% extends "base.html" %}

{% block sidebar %}
  <form class="form-inline well" method="get" role="form">
    <div class="input-group">
      <input class="form-control input-xs" name="q"
placeholder="Search..." value="{{ request.args.get('q', '') }}" />
      <span class="input-group-btn">
        <button class="btn btn-default" type="submit">Go</button>
      </span>
    </div>
  </form>
{% endblock %}

{% block content %}
  {% include "includes/list.html" %}
{% endblock %}
```

> Even though we will not explicitly pass `request` into the context, Flask will make it accessible. You can find the list of standard context variables in the Flask documentation at `http://flask.pocoo.org/docs/templating/#standard-context`.

Now we will update the `entries/index.html` and `entries/tag_detail.html` to utilize this new base template. Since the `content` block contains the list of entries, we can remove that from both templates:

```
{% extends "entries/base_entries.html" %}

{% block title %}Entries{% endblock %}

{% block content_title %}Entries{% endblock %}
```

This is how `entries/index.html` looks after changing the base template and removing the context block. Do the same to `entries/tag_detail.html`.

```
{% extends "entries/base_entries.html" %}
{% block title %}Tags{% endblock %}
{% block content_title %}Tags{% endblock %}
```

Now we need to update our view code to actually perform the search. To do this, we will create a new helper function in the blueprint named `entry_list`. This helper will be much like the `object_list` helper, but will perform extra logic to filter results based on our search inquiry. Add the `entry_list` function to the `blueprint.py`. Note how it checks the request query-string for a parameter named q. If q is present, we will return only the entries that contain the search phrase in either the title or the body:

```
from flask import request
def entry_list(template, query, **context):
    search = request.args.get('q')
    if search:
        query = query.filter(
            (Entry.body.contains(search)) |
            (Entry.title.contains(search)))
    return object_list(template, query, **context)
```

In order to utilize this functionality, modify the `index` and `tag_detail` views to call `entry_list` instead of `object_list`. The updated `index` view looks as follows:

```
@entries.route('/')
def index():
    entries = Entry.query.order_by(Entry.created_timestamp.desc())
    return entry_list('entries/index.html', entries)
```

Congratulations! You can now navigate to the entries list and perform searches using the search form.

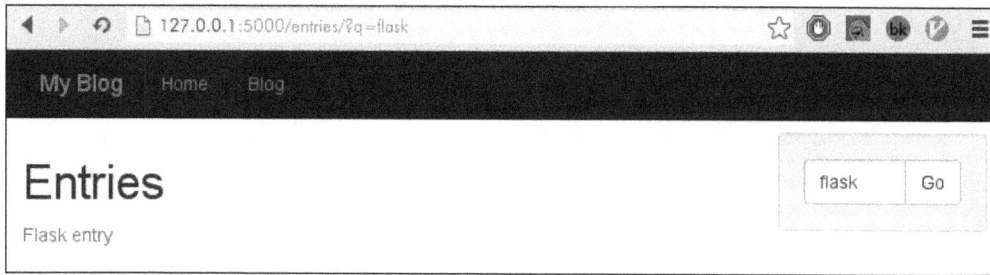

# Adding pagination links

As we discussed earlier, we would like to paginate long lists of entries so that users are not overwhelmed with extremely long lists. We have actually done all the work in the `object_list` function; the only remaining task is to add links allowing users to travel from one page of entries to the next.

Because pagination links are a feature we will use in several places, we will create the pagination `include` in our app's template directory (as opposed to the entries template directory). Create a new directory in `app/templates/` named `includes` and create a file named `page_links.html`. Since `object_list` returns us a `PaginatedQuery` object, we can utilize this object to determine, in the template, what page we are on and how many pages there are in total. In order to make the pagination links look nice, we will be using CSS classes provided by Bootstrap. Add the following content to `page_links.html`:

```
<ul class="pagination">
  <li{% if not object_list.has_prev %} class="disabled"{% endif
%}>
    {% if not object_list.has_prev %}
      <a href="./?page={{ object_list.prev_num }}">&laquo;</a>
    {% else %}
      <a href="#">&laquo;</a>
    {% endif %}
  </li>
  {% for page in object_list.iter_pages() %}
    <li>
      {% if page %}
        <a {% if page == object_list.page %}class="active" {%
endif %}href="./?page={{ page }}">{{ page }}</a>
      {% else %}
        <a class="disabled">...</a>
      {% endif %}
```

```
        </li>
    {% endfor %}
    <li{% if not object_list.has_next %} class="disabled"{% endif
%}>
        {% if object_list.has_next %}
          <a href="./?page={{ object_list.next_num }}">&raquo;</a>
        {% else %}
          <a href="#">&raquo;</a>
        {% endif %}
      </li>
    </ul>
```

Now, wherever we are displaying an object list, let's include the `page_links.html` template at the bottom of the page. Currently, the only templates we will need to update are `entries/base_entries.html` and `entries/tag_index.html`. The `content` block of `base_entries.html` looks as follows:

```
{% block content %}
    {% include "includes/list.html" %}
    {% include "includes/page_links.html" %}
{% endblock %}
```

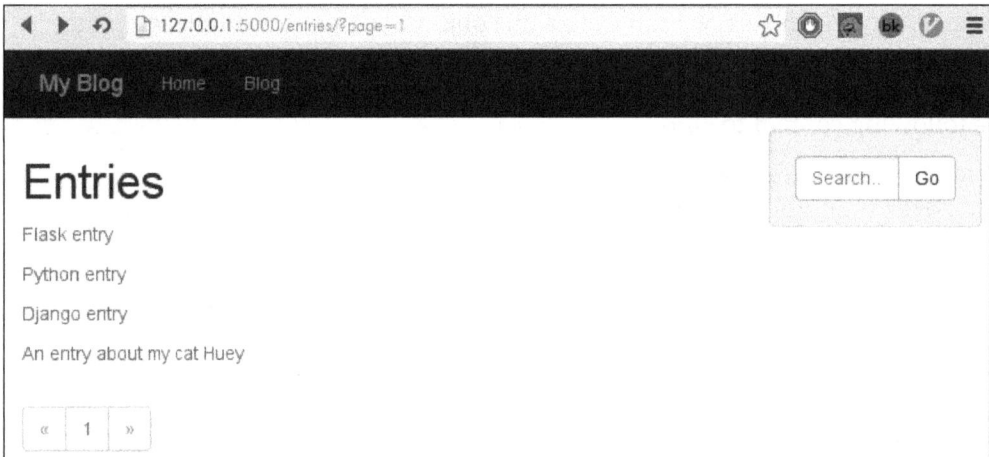

# Enhancing the blog app

Before continuing on to the next chapter, I recommend spending some time experimenting with the views and templates we created in this chapter. Here are a few ideas you might consider:

- Sort the list of tags on the entry detail view (hint: use the `sort` filter on the tag's `name` attribute).

- Remove the example code from the homepage template and add your own content.

- You may have noticed that we are displaying all entries regardless of their status. Modify the `entry_list` function and the entry `detail` view to only display `Entry` objects whose status is `STATUS_PUBLIC`.

- Experiment with different Bootstrap themes- `http://bootswatch.com` has many available for free.

- Advanced: allow multiple tags to be specified. For example, `/entries/tags/flask+python/` would only display entries that are tagged with both *flask* and *python*.

# Summary

We covered a lot of information in this chapter, and by now you should be familiar with the process of creating views and templates. We learned how to render Jinja2 templates and how to pass data from the view into the template context. We also learned how to modify context data within the template, using Jinja2 tags and filters. In the second half of the chapter, we designed a URL structure for our site and translated it into Flask views. We added a simple full-text search feature to the site, and wrapped up by adding pagination links to our lists of entries and tags.

In the next chapter, we will learn how to create and edit blog entries through the website using **Forms**. We will learn how to process and validate user input, then save the changes to the database. We will also add a photo-uploading feature so we can embed images in our blog entries.

# 4
# Forms and Validation

In this chapter, we will learn how to use forms to modify the content on our blog directly through the site. This will be a fun chapter because we will be adding all sorts of new ways to interact with our site. We will create forms for working with the Entry model, learn how to receive and validate user data, and finally update the values in the database. Form processing and validation will be handled by the popular **WTForms** library. We will continue building out views and templates to support these new forms, learning a few new Jinja2 tricks along the way.

In this chapter we shall:

- Install WTForms and create a form for working with the Entry model
- Write views to validate and process form data, and persist changes to the database
- Create templates to display forms and validation errors
- Use Jinja2 macros to encapsulate complex template logic
- Display flash messages to the user
- Create an image uploader and learn how to securely handle file uploads
- Learn how to store and serve static assets, such as JavaScript, stylesheets and image uploads

## Getting started with WTForms

**WTForms** is a popular choice for form processing and validation in the Flask community. It uses a declarative approach to building forms (similar to how we defined our SQLAlchemy models), and supports a variety of different field types and validators.

> At the time of writing this book, WTForms 2.0 is still a development release, but should be the official release shortly. For that reason we will be using version 2.0 in this book.

Let's get started by installing WTForms into our blog project `virtualenv`:

```
(blog) $ pip install "wtforms>=2.0"
Successfully installed wtforms
Cleaning up...
```

We can verify that the installation succeeded by opening up a shell and checking the project version:

```
(blog) $ ./manage.py shell
In [1]: import wtforms

In [2]: wtforms.__version__
Out[2]: '2.0dev'
```

My version shows the development release since 2.0 has not been officially released yet.

# Defining a form for the Entry model

Our goal is to be able to create and edit blog entries directly through our site, so the first question we need to answer is—How will we input the data for our new entries? The answer, of course, is by using forms. Forms are a part of the HTML standard, which allows us to use free-form text inputs, large multi-line text boxes, drop-down selects, checkboxes, radio buttons, and more. When a user submits a form, the form specifies a URL that will receive the form data. That URL can then process the data and then respond in any way it likes.

For blog entries, let's keep it simple with three fields:

- `Title`, displayed as a simple text input
- `Body`, displayed as a large free-form textbox
- `Status`, which will be displayed as drop-down select

Inside the `entries` directory, create a new Python file named `forms.py`. We will be defining a simple form class that will contain these fields. Open `forms.py` and add the following code:

```python
import wtforms

from models import Entry

class EntryForm(wtforms.Form):
    title = wtforms.StringField('Title')
    body = wtforms.TextAreaField('Body')
    status = wtforms.SelectField(
        'Entry status',
        choices=(
            (Entry.STATUS_PUBLIC, 'Public'),
            (Entry.STATUS_DRAFT, 'Draft')),
        coerce=int)
```

This should look pretty similar to our model definition. Note that we're using the names of the columns in our model as the names for the fields in our form: this will allow WTForms to automatically copy data between the Entry model fields and the form fields.

The first two fields, `title` and `body`, both specify a single argument: the label that will be displayed when the form is rendered. The `status` field contains a label as well as two additional parameters: `choices` and `coerce`. The `choices` parameter consists of a list of 2-tuples where the first value is the actual value we are interested in storing and the second value is a user-friendly representation. The second parameter, `coerce`, will convert the value from the form to an integer (by default, it would be treated as a string, which we do not want).

# A form with a view

In order to start using this form, we need to create a view that will display the form and accept data when it is submitted. To do this, let's open the entries blueprint module and define a new URL route to handle entry creation. At the top of the `blueprint.py` file, we need to import the `EntryForm` class from the `forms` module:

```python
from app import db
from helpers import object_list
from models import Entry, Tag
from entries.forms import EntryForm
```

Then, above the definition for the `detail` view, we will add a new view named `create` that will be accessed by navigating to `/entries/create/`. The reason we must put it above the `detail` view is because Flask will search your URL routes in the order in which they are defined. Since `/entries/create/` looks very much like an entry detail URL (imagine the title of the entry was `create`), if the detail route is defined first, Flask will stop there and never reach the create route.

In our create view, we will simply instantiate the form and pass it into the template context. Add the following view definition:

```
@entries.route('/create/')
def create():
    form = EntryForm()
    return render_template('entries/create.html', form=form)
```

Before we add code to save the new entries to the database, let's build a template and see what our form looks like. We will then circle back and add the code to validate the form data and create the new entry.

# The create.html template

Let's build a basic template for our new form. Create a new template named `create.html` alongside the other entry templates. The path to this file, relative to the app directory, should be `entries/templates/entries/create.html`. We will extend the base template and override the content block to display our form. Since we are using bootstrap, we will use special CSS classes to make our form look nice. Add the following HTML code:

```
{% extends "base.html" %}

{% block title %}Create new entry{% endblock %}

{% block content_title %}Create new entry{% endblock %}

{% block content %}
  <form action="{{ url_for('entries.create') }}" class="form form-
horizontal" method="post">
    {% for field in form %}
      <div class="form-group">
        {{ field.label(class='col-sm-3 control-label') }}
        <div class="col-sm-9">
          {{ field(class='form-control') }}
        </div>
      </div>
```

```
    {% endfor %}
    <div class="form-group">
      <div class="col-sm-offset-3 col-sm-9">
        <button type="submit" class="btn btn-
default">Create</button>
        <a class="btn" href="{{ url_for('entries.index')
}}">Cancel</a>
      </div>
    </div>
  </form>
{% endblock %}
```

By iterating over the form, which we passed into the context, we can render each individual field. To render the field, we first render the field's label by simply calling field.label() and passing in the desired CSS class. Similarly, to render the field, we call field(), again passing in the CSS class. Also note that, in addition to a submit button, we've added a Cancel link that will return the user to the entries list.

Start the development server and navigate to http://127.0.0.1:5000/entries/ create/ to view the following form:

Try submitting the form. When you click the **Create** button, you should see the following error message:

The reason you are seeing this message is because, by default, Flask views will only respond to HTTP GET requests. When we submit our form, the browser sends a POST request, which our view does not currently accept. Let's return to the create view and add the code to correctly handle the POST requests.

> Whenever a form makes changes to the data (creates, edits, or deletes something), that form should specify the POST method. Other forms, such as our search form, which do not make any changes, should use the GET method. Additionally, when a form is submitted using the GET method, the form data is submitted as part of the query-string.

# Handling form submissions

Before we modify our view, let's add a helper method to our EntryForm that we will use to copy data from the form into our Entry object. Open forms.py and make the following additions:

```
class EntryForm(wtforms.Form):
    ...
    def save_entry(self, entry):
        self.populate_obj(entry)
        entry.generate_slug()
        return entry
```

This helper method will populate the entry we pass in with the form data, re-generate the entry's slug based on the title, and then return the entry object.

Now that the form is configured to populate our `Entry` models, we can modify the view to accept and handle the POST requests. We will be using two new Flask helpers, so modify the imports at the top of `blueprint.py`, adding `redirect` and `url_for`:

```
from flask import Blueprint, redirect, render_template, request,
url_for
```

Once you've added the imports, update the following changes to the `create` view in `blueprint.py`:

```
from app import db
@entries.route('/create/', methods=['GET', 'POST'])
def create():
    if request.method == 'POST':
        form = EntryForm(request.form)
        if form.validate():
            entry = form.save_entry(Entry())
            db.session.add(entry)
            db.session.commit()
            return redirect(url_for('entries.detail', slug=entry.
slug))
    else:
        form = EntryForm()

    return render_template('entries/create.html', form=form)
```

This is quite a bit of new code, so let's take a closer look at what's happening. To begin with, we've added a parameter to the route decorator indicating that this view accepts both GET and POST requests. This will get rid of the **Method Not Allowed** error when we submit the form.

In the body of the view, we are now checking the `request` method and based on that we do one of two things. Let's look at the 'else' clause first. This branch of code will execute when we receive a GET request, such as when someone opens their browser and navigates to the `/entries/create/` page. When this happens, we simply want to display an HTML page containing the form, so we will instantiate a form and pass it into the template context.

In the event this is a POST request, which will happen when someone submits the form, we want to instantiate the `EntryForm` and pass in the raw form data. Flask stores the raw POST data in the special attribute `request.form`, which is a dictionary-like object. WTForms knows how to interpret the raw form data and map it to the fields we defined.

After instantiating our form with the raw form data, we then need to check and ensure that the form is valid by calling `form.validate()`. If the form fails to validate for some reason, we will simply pass the invalid form into the context and render the template. A bit later you will see how we can display error messages to the user when there is a problem with their form submission.

If the form validates, we can finally proceed with saving the entry. To do this, we will call our `save_entry` helper method, passing in a fresh `entry` instance. WTForms will populate the `Entry` object with form data, then return it back to us, where we add it to the database session, commit, and redirect. The redirect helper will issue an HTTP 302 redirect, sending the user's browser from `/entries/create/` to the detail page of the newly-created blog post.

Open up your browser and give it a try.

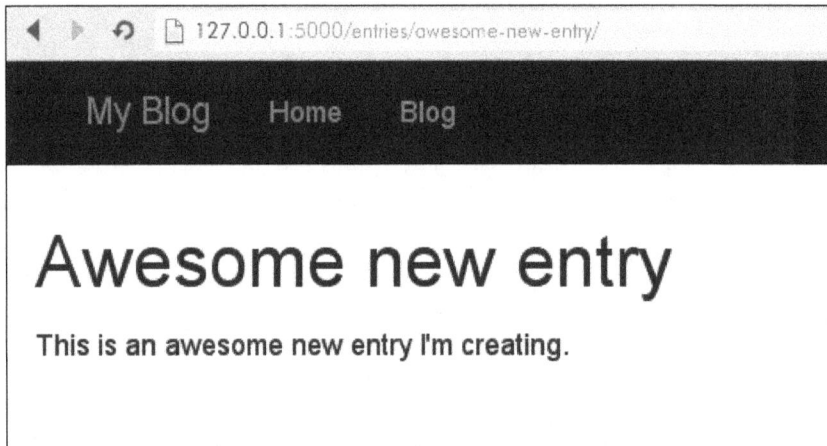

## Validating input and displaying error messages

There is one glaring problem with our form: right now there is nothing to prevent us from accidentally submitting an empty blog entry. To ensure that we have a title and content when saving, we need to use a WTForm object called a validator. Validators are rules that are applied to the form data, and WTForms ships with a number of useful validators. Some of the more commonly-used validators are listed as follows:

- `DataRequired`: this field cannot be blank
- `Length(min=?, max=?)`: verify that the length of the data entered either exceeds the minimum, or does not exceed the maximum

- `NumberRange(min=?, max=?)`: verify that the number entered is within the given range
- `Email`: verify that the data is a valid email address
- `URL`: verify that the data entered is a valid URL
- `AnyOf(values=?)`: verify that the data entered is equal to one of the provided values
- `NoneOf(values=?)`: verify that the data entered is not equal to any of the provided values

For the blog entry form, we will just be using the `DataRequired` validator to ensure that Entries cannot be created without a title or body content. Let's open `forms.py` and add the validators to our form definition. Altogether, our forms module should look a follows:

```python
import wtforms
from wtforms.validators import DataRequired

from models import Entry


class EntryForm(wtforms.Form):
    title = wtforms.StringField(
        'Title',
        validators=[DataRequired()])
    body = wtforms.TextAreaField(
        'Body',
        validators=[DataRequired()])
    status = wtforms.SelectField(
        'Entry status',
        choices=(
            (Entry.STATUS_PUBLIC, 'Public'),
            (Entry.STATUS_DRAFT, 'Draft')),
        coerce=int)

    def save_entry(self, entry):
        self.populate_obj(entry)
        entry.generate_slug()
        return entry
```

Start the development server and now try to submit an empty form. As you might expect, it will fail to save since the call to `form.validate()` returns `False`. Unfortunately, there is no indication on the front-end why our form is not getting saved. Luckily, WTForms will make the validation errors available to us in the template, and all we need to do is modify our template to display them.

To display validation errors we will be using several bootstrap CSS classes and constructions, but the end result will look very nice, as seen in the following screenshot:

## Create new entry

| | |
|---|---|
| **Title** | ⚠ |
| | This field is required. |
| **Body** | ⚠ |
| | This field is required. |
| **Entry status** | Public ▼ |
| | Create   Cancel |

Make the following changes to the field display code in the `create.html` template:

```
{% for field in form %}
  <div class="form-group{% if field.errors %} has-error has-feedback{%
endif %}">
    {{ field.label(class='col-sm-3 control-label') }}
    <div class="col-sm-9">
      {{ field(class='form-control') }}
      {% if field.errors %}
        <span class="glyphicon glyphicon-warning-sign form-control-
feedback"></span>
      {% endif %}
      {% for error in field.errors %}<span class="help-block">{{ error
}}</span>{% endfor %}
```

```
    </div>
  </div>
{% endfor %}
```

We are checking whether the field has any errors by looking at the `field.errors` attribute. If there are any errors, then we do the following things:

- Add a CSS class to the `form-group` div
- Add a special icon indicating there is an error
- Display each error in a `<span>` beneath the form field. Since `field.errors` is a list and may contain multiple validation errors, we will iterate through these using a for loop

You are now able to create valid blog entries using a form, which also performs a little validation to ensure that you do not submit blank forms. In the next section, we will describe how to re-use this same form for editing existing entries.

# Editing existing entries

Believe it or not, we can actually use the same form we used for creating entries to edit existing ones. We will only need to make some slight changes to the view and template logic, so let's get started.

In order to edit entries, we will need a view, so we will need a URL. Because the view needs to know which entry we are editing, it will be important to convey that as part of the URL structure, and for that reason we will set up the `edit` view at `/entries/<slug>/edit/`. Open `entries/blueprint.py` and, below the detail view, add the following code for the `edit` view. Note the similarities to the `create` view:

```
@entries.route('/<slug>/edit/', methods=['GET', 'POST'])
def edit(slug):
    entry = Entry.query.filter(Entry.slug == slug).first_or_404()
    if request.method == 'POST':
        form = EntryForm(request.form, obj=entry)
        if form.validate():
            entry = form.save_entry(entry)
            db.session.add(entry)
            db.session.commit()
            return redirect(url_for('entries.detail',
slug=entry.slug))
    else:
```

```
form = EntryForm(obj=entry)

return render_template('entries/edit.html', entry=entry,
form=form)
```

Just as we did with the `create` view, we check the `request` method and, based on that, we will either validate and process the form, or simply instantiate it and pass it to the template.

The biggest difference is in how we are instantiating the `EntryForm`. We pass it an additional parameter, `obj=entry`. When WTForms receives an `obj` parameter, it will attempt to pre-populate the form fields with values taken from `obj` (in this case, our blog entry).

We are also passing an additional value into the template context, the entry that we are editing. We will do this so we can display the title of the entry to the user; in this way, we can make the **Cancel** button of the form link back to the entry detail view.

# The edit.html template

As you might guess, the `edit.html` template will be almost identical to `create.html`. Due to the complexity of the field rendering logic, it seems like a bad idea to copy-and-paste all that code. If we ever decided to change the display of the form fields, we would find ourselves touching multiple files, which should always be a big red flag.

To avoid this, we will be using a powerful Jinja2 feature called macros to render our fields. The field rendering code will be defined in a macro and then, wherever we wish to render a field, we will just call our macro instead. This makes it really easy to make changes to the way our fields are styled.

> Macros are a feature of Jinja2 that allow you to treat a section of a template like a function so it can be called multiple times with different arguments and produce largely similar HTML. You can view more on the Jinja documentation site: `http://jinja.pocoo.org/docs/dev/templates/`

Since this macro is going to be useful for any form field we might wish to display, we will put it in our app's template directory. Inside the app's template directory, create a new directory named `macros` and add a field `form_field.html`. Relative to the app directory, the path to this file is `templates/macros/form_field.html`. Add the following code:

```
{% macro form_field(field) %}
  <div class="form-group{% if field.errors %} has-error has-
feedback{% endif %}">
    {{ field.label(class='col-sm-3 control-label') }}
    <div class="col-sm-9">
      {{ field(class='form-control', **kwargs) }}
      {% if field.errors %}<span class="glyphicon glyphicon-
warning-sign form-control-feedback"></span>{% endif %}
      {% for error in field.errors %}<span class="help-block">{{
error }}</span>{% endfor %}
    </div>
  </div>
{% endmacro %}
```

For the most part, we have simply copied and pasted the field rendering code from our `create` template but there are a couple of differences I'd like to point out:

- The template begins with a `macro` template tag that defines the name of the `macro` and any arguments that it accepts.

- When we render the field, we are passing in `**kwargs`. WTForms fields can accept arbitrary keyword arguments, which are then translated into attributes on the HTML tag. While we are not currently going to make use of this, we will be using it in later chapters.

- We indicate the end of a macro with the `endmacro` tag.

Now let's update `create.html` to make use of the new macro. In order to use the macro, we must first `import` it. Then we can replace all the field markup with a simple call to the macro. With the changes, the `create.html` template should look like this:

```
{% extends "base.html" %}
{% from "macros/form_field.html" import form_field %}

{% block title %}Create new entry{% endblock %}

{% block content_title %}Create new entry{% endblock %}

{% block content %}
```

```
    <form action="{{ url_for('entries.create') }}" class="form form-
horizontal" method="post">
      {% for field in form %}
        {{ form_field(field) }}
      {% endfor %}
      <div class="form-group">
        <div class="col-sm-offset-3 col-sm-9">
          <button type="submit" class="btn btn-
default">Create</button>
          <a class="btn" href="{{ url_for('entries.index')
}}">Cancel</a>
        </div>
      </div>
    </form>
{% endblock %}
```

With that out of the way, we can proceed to creating our `edit.html` template. It will look almost identical to the `create` template, except we will display text in the `app/entries/templates/entries` directory to indicate to the user that they are editing an existing entry:

```
{% extends "base.html" %}
{% from "macros/form_field.html" import form_field %}

{% block title %}Edit {{ entry.title }}{% endblock %}

{% block content_title %}Edit {{ entry.title }}{% endblock %}

{% block content %}
    <form action="{{ url_for('entries.edit', slug=entry.slug) }}"
class="form form-horizontal" method="post">
      {% for field in form %}
        {{ form_field(field) }}
      {% endfor %}
      <div class="form-group">
        <div class="col-sm-offset-3 col-sm-9">
          <button type="submit" class="btn btn-default">Save</button>
          <a class="btn" href="{{ url_for('entries.detail', slug=entry.
slug) }}">Cancel</a>
        </div>
      </div>
    </form>
{% endblock %}
```

To wrap things up, on the entry detail page let's add a link in the sidebar that will take us to the Edit page. Add the following link to the sidebar in detail.html:

```
<a href="{{ url_for('entries.edit', slug=entry.slug) }}">Edit</a>
```

# Deleting entries

To round out this section, we will add a view for deleting entries. We will design this view so that, when the user goes to delete an entry, they are taken to a confirmation page. Only by submitting the confirmation form (a POST request) will they actually be able to delete the entry. Because this form does not require any fields, we do not need a special WTForms class and can just create it using HTML.

Create a template named delete.html alongside the create.html and edit.html templates, and add the following HTML:

```
{% extends "base.html" %}

{% block title %}{{ entry.title }}{% endblock %}

{% block content_title %}{{ entry.title }}{% endblock %}

{% block content %}
  <form action="{{ url_for('entries.delete', slug=entry.slug) }}"
method="post">
    <fieldset>
      <legend>Delete this entry?</legend>
      <button class="btn btn-danger" type="submit">Delete</button>
      <a class="btn" href="{{ url_for('entries.detail', slug=entry.
slug) }}">Cancel</a>
    </fieldset>
  </form>
{% endblock %}
```

Now we need to define the entries.delete view. Like the edit view, the URL for deleting an entry needs the entry slug as part of the URL structure. For that reason, we will be using /entries/<slug>/delete/.

When the form is submitted, we could simply remove the entry from the database but in my experience I have usually come to regret deleting content permanently. Instead of actually deleting the entry from the database, we will be giving it a _ DELETED status; we will change its status to STATUS_DELETED. We will then modify our views so that entries with this status never appear on any part of the site. For all intents and purposes, the entry is gone but, should we ever need it again, we can retrieve it from the database. Add the following view code below the edit view:

```
@entries.route('/<slug>/delete/', methods=['GET', 'POST'])
def delete(slug):
    entry = Entry.query.filter(Entry.slug == slug).first_or_404()
    if request.method == 'POST':
        entry.status = Entry.STATUS_DELETED
        db.session.add(entry)
        db.session.commit()
        return redirect(url_for('entries.index'))

    return render_template('entries/delete.html', entry=entry)
```

We will also need to add STATUS_DELETED to the Entries model in model.py:

```
class Entry(db.Model):
    STATUS_PUBLIC = 0
    STATUS_DRAFT = 1
    STATUS_DELETED = 2
```

As we did with the Edit link, take a moment and add a delete link to the detail view sidebar as well.

# Cleaning up

Let's take a moment to refactor our blueprint. Since we do not want to display deleted entries on the site, we will need to make sure we filter our Entries by status. Additionally, looking at the detail, edit and delete views, I see three instances where we have copied and pasted the code to query an entry by slug. Let's move that into a helper function as well.

To start with, let's update the entry_list helper to filter for Entries that are either public or drafts.

> In the next chapter, we will be adding log-in functionality to the site. Once we have that, we will add logic to display draft entries only to the users who created them.

```
def entry_list(template, query, **context):
    valid_statuses = (Entry.STATUS_PUBLIC, Entry.STATUS_DRAFT)
    query = query.filter(Entry.status.in_(valid_statuses))
    if request.args.get('q'):
        search = request.args['q']
        query = query.filter(
            (Entry.body.contains(search)) |
            (Entry.title.contains(search)))

    return object_list(template, query, **context)
```

We can now be confident that anywhere we display lists of entries, no deleted entries will show up.

Now let's add a new helper to retrieve an `Entry` by its slug. If the entry cannot be found, we will return a 404. Add the following code below `entry_list`:

```
def get_entry_or_404(slug):
    valid_statuses = (Entry.STATUS_PUBLIC, Entry.STATUS_DRAFT) (Entry.
query
        .filter(
            (Entry.slug == slug) &
            (Entry.status.in_(valid_statuses)))
        .first_or_404())
```

Replace the call to `Entry.query.filter()` in the `detail`, `edit`, and `delete` views with a call to `get_entry_or_404`. The following is the updated detail view:

```
@entries.route('/<slug>/')
def detail(slug):
    entry = get_entry_or_404(slug)
    return render_template('entries/detail.html', entry=entry)
```

# Using flash messages

When a user performs an action on a site, it is common to display a one-time message on the subsequent page-load indicating that their action has succeeded. These are called flash messages and Flask comes with a helper for displaying them. In order to get started using flash messages, we need to take a brief detour to our `config` module where we will be adding a secret key. The secret key is necessary because flash messages are stored in the session, which in turn is stored as an encrypted cookie. To securely encrypt this data, Flask needs a key.

Open `config.py` and add a secret key. It can be a phrase, random characters, whatever you like:

```
class Configuration(object):
    APPLICATION_DIR = current_directory
    DEBUG = True
    SECRET_KEY = 'flask is fun!'  # Create a unique key for your app.
    SQLALCHEMY_DATABASE_URI = 'sqlite:///%s/blog.db' %
APPLICATION_DIR
```

Now, wherever we have the user performing an action, we want to flash them a message indicating that their action succeeded. This means we will be adding a message to the `create`, `edit`, and `delete` views. Open up the entries blueprint and add the flash function to the list of flask imports at the top of the module:

```
from flask import Blueprint, flash, redirect, render_template,
request, url_for
```

Then, in each of the appropriate views, let's call `flash` with a helpful message. The call should occur right before we redirect:

```
def create():
        ...
            db.session.commit()
            flash('Entry "%s" created successfully.' % entry.title,
'success')
            return redirect(url_for('entries.detail', slug=entry.
slug))
        ...

def edit(slug):
        ...
        db.session.commit()
        flash('Entry "%s" has been saved.' % entry.title, 'success')
        return redirect(url_for('entries.detail', slug=entry.slug))
        ...

def delete(slug):
        ...
        db.session.commit()
        flash('Entry "%s" has been deleted.' % entry.title, 'success')
        return redirect(url_for('entries.index'))
        ...
```

# Displaying flash messages in the template

Because we do not always know which page we will be on when we need to display a flash message, it is a standard practice to add the display logic to the base template. Flask provides a Jinja2 function `get_flashed_messages` that will return us a list of any pending messages to display.

Open `base.html` and add the following code. I have placed mine between the `content_title` block and the `content` block:

```
<h1>{% block content_title %}{% endblock %}</h1>
{% for category, message in get_flashed_messages(with_categories=true)
%}
  <div class="alert alert-dismissable alert-{{ category }}">
    <button type="button" class="close" data-dismiss="alert">&times;</
button>
    {{ message }}
  </div>
{% endfor %}
{% block content %}{% endblock %}
```

Let's give it a try! Start the development server and try adding a new entry. Upon saving, you should be redirected to your new entry and see a helpful message as seen in the following screenshot:

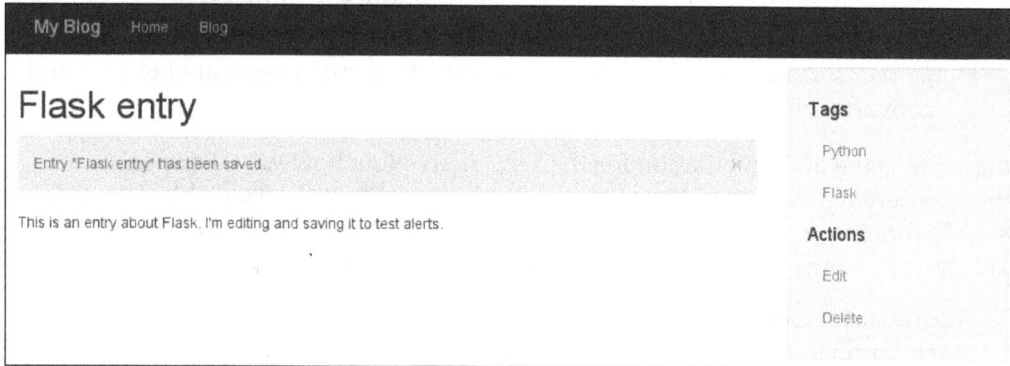

# Saving and modifying tags on posts

We have covered how to save and modify tags on our entries. One of the most common approaches to managing tags is to use a comma-separated text input, so we might list the tags as *Python, Flask, Web-development*. With WTForms this seems pretty straightforward, since we would just use a `StringField`. The fact that we are dealing with a database relationship, though, means that at some point we need to do some processing to convert between `Tag` models and a comma-separated string.

While there are many ways we could accomplish this, we will implement a custom field class `TagField`, which will encapsulate all the logic for translating between comma-separated tag names and `Tag` model instances.

> Another option would be to create a *property* on the `Entry` model. A property looks like a normal object attribute, but it is actually a combination of getter and (sometimes) setter methods. Since WTForms can automatically work with our model attributes, this means that, if we implement our translation logic in the getter and setter, WTForms will just work.

Let's start by defining our tag field class. There are two important methods we need to override:

* `_value()`: converts the list of `Tag` instances into a comma-separated list of tag names
* `process_formdata(valuelist)`: accepts the comma-separated tag list and converts it into a list of `Tag` instances

Following is the implementation for the `TagField`. Note how we take special care when processing user input to not create duplicate rows in the `Tag` table. We are also using Python's `set()` data-type to eliminate possible duplicates in the user input. Add the following class to `forms.py` above the `EntryForm`:

```python
from models import Tag
class TagField(wtforms.StringField):
    def _value(self):
        if self.data:
            # Display tags as a comma-separated list.
            return ', '.join([tag.name for tag in self.data])
        return ''

    def get_tags_from_string(self, tag_string):
```

```
            raw_tags = tag_string.split(',')

            # Filter out any empty tag names.
            tag_names = [name.strip() for name in raw_tags if name.
strip()]

            # Query the database and retrieve any tags we have already
saved.
            existing_tags = Tag.query.filter(Tag.name.in_(tag_names))

            # Determine which tag names are new.
            new_names = set(tag_names) - set([tag.name for tag in
existing_tags])

            # Create a list of unsaved Tag instances for the new tags.
            new_tags = [Tag(name=name) for name in new_names]

            # Return all the existing tags + all the new, unsaved tags.
            return list(existing_tags) + new_tags

        def process_formdata(self, valuelist):
            if valuelist:
                self.data = self.get_tags_from_string(valuelist[0])
            else:
                self.data = []
```

Now all that is left is to add the field to the `EntryForm`. Add the following field below the `status` field. Note the use of the `description` keyword argument:

```
    class EntryForm(wtforms.Form):
        ...
        tags = TagField(
            'Tags',
            description='Separate multiple tags with commas.')
```

In order to display this helpful `description` text, let's make a quick modification to the `form_field` macro:

```
{% macro form_field(field) %}
  <div class="form-group{% if field.errors %} has-error has-feedback{%
endif %}">
    {{ field.label(class='col-sm-3 control-label') }}
    <div class="col-sm-9">
      {{ field(class='form-control', **kwargs) }}
```

```
        {% if field.errors %}<span class="glyphicon glyphicon-warning-
sign form-control-feedback"></span>{% endif %}
        {% if field.description %}<span class="help-block">{{ field.
description|safe }}</span>{% endif %}
        {% for error in field.errors %}<span class="help-block">{{ error
}}</span>{% endfor %}
    </div>
  </div>
{% endmacro %}
```

Start the development server and experiment by saving a few tags. Your form should look something like the following screenshot:

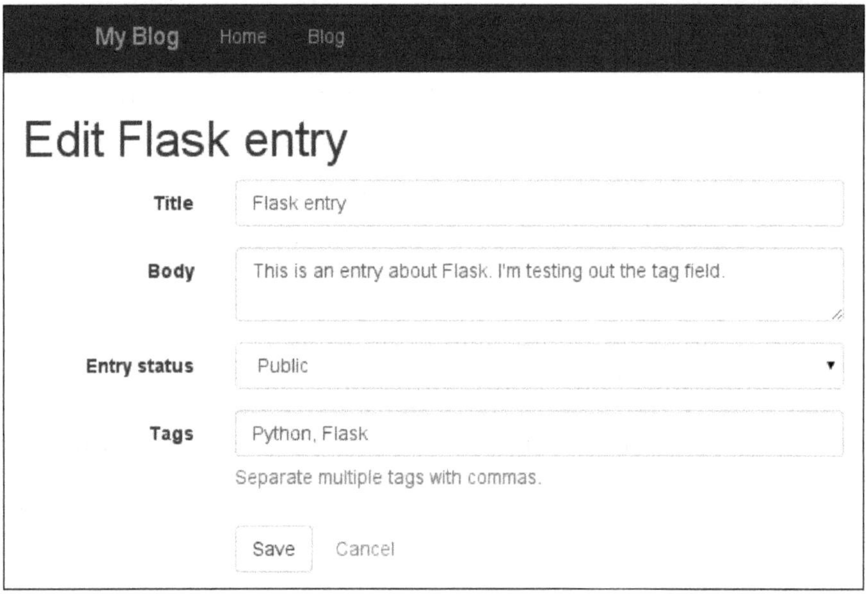

# Image uploads

We'll round out the chapter on form processing by adding an image-uploading feature to the site. This feature will be a simple view that accepts an image file and stores it on the server in an uploads directory. This will make it easy to display images on our blog entries.

The first step will be to create a form for handling our image uploads. Alongside `EntryForm`, let's add a new form called `ImageForm`. This form will be very simple and contain a single file input. We will use a custom validator to ensure that the uploaded file is a valid image. Add the following code to `forms.py`:

```
class ImageForm(wtforms.Form):
    file = wtforms.FileField('Image file')
```

Before we add a view to save the form, we need to know where we are going to save the file. Typically, resources for an app—such as images, JavaScript, and stylesheets—are served out of a single directory called `static`. Common practice is to then over-ride the path to this directory in your web server so it can transfer this file without having to go through a Python intermediary, making access much faster. We make use of this usage of the `static` directory to store our image uploads. In the blog project's app directory, let's create a new directory named `static` and a subdirectory `images`:

```
(blog) $ cd ~/projects/blog/blog/app
(blog) $ mkdir -p static/images
```

Now let's add a new value to our configuration file so we can easily reference the path to our images on-disk. This simplifies our code in the long run should we ever choose to change this location. Open `config.py` and add the following value:

```
class Configuration(object):
    ...
    STATIC_DIR = os.path.join(APPLICATION_DIR, 'static')
    IMAGES_DIR = os.path.join(STATIC_DIR, 'images')
```

# Processing file uploads

We are now ready to create a view for processing the image upload. The logic will be very similar to our other form processing views with the exception that, after validating the form, we will save the uploaded file to disk. Since these images are intended for use in our blog entries, I am adding the view to the entries blueprint, accessible at `/entries/image-upload/`.

We need to import our new form along with other helpers. Open `blueprint.py` and add the following imports to the top of the module:

```
import os

from flask import Blueprint, flash, redirect, render_template,
request, url_for
from werkzeug import secure_filename

from app import app, db
from helpers import object_list
from models import Entry, Tag
from entries.forms import EntryForm, ImageForm
```

At the top of the list of views, let's add the new `image-upload` view. It is important that it appears before the `detail` view, otherwise Flask will incorrectly treat `/image-upload/` as the slug of a blog entry. Add the following view definition:

```
@entries.route('/image-upload/', methods=['GET', 'POST'])
def image_upload():
    if request.method == 'POST':
        form = ImageForm(request.form)
        if form.validate():
            image_file = request.files['file']
            filename = os.path.join(app.config['IMAGES_DIR'],
                               secure_filename(image_file.
filename))
            image_file.save(filename)
            flash('Saved %s' % os.path.basename(filename), 'success')
            return redirect(url_for('entries.index'))
    else:
        form = ImageForm()

    return render_template('entries/image_upload.html', form=form)
```

Most of the code here probably looks familiar to you, the notable exception being the use of `request.files` and `secure_filename`. When a file is uploaded, Flask will store it in `request.files`, which is a special dictionary keyed by the name of the form field. We do some path joining using `secure_filename` to prevent malicious filenames and to generate the correct path to the `static/images` directory, and then save the uploaded file to disk. It is that easy.

# The image upload template

Let's create a simple template for our image upload form. Create a file in the entries template directory named `image_upload.html` and add the following code:

```
{% extends "base.html" %}
{% from "macros/form_field.html" import form_field %}

{% block title %}Upload an image{% endblock %}

{% block content_title %}Upload an image{% endblock %}

{% block content %}
  <form action="{{ url_for('entries.image_upload') }}"
enctype="multipart/form-data" method="post">
    {% for field in form %}
      {{ form_field(field) }}
    {% endfor %}
    <div class="form-group">
      <div class="col-sm-offset-3 col-sm-9">
        <button type="submit" class="btn btn-
default">Upload</button>
        <a class="btn" href="{{ url_for('entries.index')
}}">Cancel</a>
      </div>
    </div>
  </form>
{% endblock %}
```

In order for Flask to process our uploaded file, we must specify `enctype="multipart/form-data"` when defining our `<form>` element. This is a very common mistake, so I will repeat again: whenever you are accepting file uploads, your form element must specify `enctype="multipart/form-data"`.

Go ahead and try out the image uploader. You should see your uploaded files appear in the `static/images/directory` in your app. You can also view the image in your browser by navigating to `http://127.0.0.1:5000/static/images/the-file-name.jpg`.

# Serving static files

Flask will automatically serve up files from our /static/ directory. When we deploy our site in *Chapter 10, Deploying Your Application*, we will use the **Nginx** web server to serve static assets but, for local development, Flask makes things really easy.

In addition to our image uploads, let's also serve our site's JavaScript and stylesheets from /static/. Download jQuery and Bootstrap and place the JavaScript files (jquery-<version>.min.js and bootstrap.min.js) in static/js. Place the minified bootstrap CSS file (bootstrap.min.css) in static/css. Bootstrap also comes with some special fonts that are used for icons. Copy the bootstrap fonts directory into the static directory as well. You should now have four directories inside your application's static directory: css, fonts, images and js, each containing the relevant files:

```
(blog) $ cd static/ && find . -type f
./fonts/glyphicons-halflings-regular.woff
./fonts/glyphicons-halflings-regular.ttf
./fonts/glyphicons-halflings-regular.eot
./fonts/glyphicons-halflings-regular.svg
./images/2012-07-17_16.18.18.jpg
./js/jquery-1.10.2.min.js
./js/bootstrap.min.js
./css/bootstrap.min.css
```

In order to point our base template at the local versions of these files, we will use the url_for helper to generate the correct URL. Open base.html and remove the old stylesheet and JavaScript tags, replacing them with the local version:

```
<head>
  <meta charset="utf-8">
  <title>{% block title %}{% endblock %} | My Blog</title>

  <link rel="stylesheet" href="{{="{{ url_for('static', filename='css/
bootstrap.min.css') }}">
  <style type="text/css">
    body { padding-top: 60px; }
  </style>
  {% block extra_styles %}{% endblock %}

  <script src="{{ url_for('static', filename='js/jquery-1.10.2.min.
js') }}"></script>
```

```
    <script src="{{ url_for('static', filename='js/bootstrap.min.js')
}}"></script>
    {% block extra_scripts %}{% endblock %}
</head>
```

If you like, you can create a `site.css` file in the `static/css` directory and replace the `<style>` tag with a link to `site.css`.

# Summary

In this chapter, we added a variety of new ways to interact with the site. It is now possible to create and modify content directly through the site. We discussed how to create object-oriented forms with WTForms, including processing and validating the form data from the view, as well as writing that form data to the database. We also created templates to display forms and validation errors and used Jinja2 macros to remove repetitive code to make the code more modular. We were then able to display single-use flash messages to the user when they perform an action. Finally we also explained how to handle file uploads using WTForms and Flask, and to serve static assets, such as JavaScript, stylesheets, and image uploads.

Before jumping into the next chapter, take some time to experiment with the new features we added to the site. Here are some ideas for ways you can improve on what we've built in this chapter:

* Add a header link to the image upload form.
* In the image upload view, validate that the file's extension is a recognized image extension (.png, .jpg, .gif).
* Add a read-only StringField to display the Entry's slug.
* Our tag index view will show tags that have zero entries associated with them (which might be the case if we added a tag, then removed it from an entry). Improve the query to only list tags with one or more associated entries. Hint: `Tag.query.join(entry_tags).distinct()`.
* Display the number of entries associated with a tag in the tag index. Advanced: do it in a single query.
* Advanced: Create an Image model and views for creating, editing, and deleting images.

In the next chapter, we will add authentication to our site so that only trusted users can create and modify content. We will build a model to represent blog authors, add log-in/log-out forms, and prevent unauthenticated users from accessing certain areas of the site.

# 5

# Authenticating Users

In this chapter, we will add user authentication to our site. Being able to distinguish one user from another allows us to develop an entirely new class of features. For instance, we will see how to restrict access to the create, edit, and delete views, preventing anonymous users from tampering with site content. We can also display a user's draft posts to them, but hide them from everyone else. This chapter will cover the practical aspects of adding an authentication layer to the site, and wrap up with a discussion of how to use sessions to track anonymous users as well.

In this chapter we shall:

- Create a database model to represent users
- Install Flask-Login and add the LoginManager helper to our site
- Learn to securely store and validate passwords using cryptographic hash functions
- Build forms and views for logging users in and out of the site
- See how to reference the logged-in user in views and templates
- Limit access to views to logged-in users
- Add an author foreign key to the Entry model
- Use the Flask session object to track any visitor to the site

# Creating a user model

The first step in building our authentication system will be to create a database model representing an individual user account. We will store the user's login credentials, along with some additional information such as the user's display name, and their account creation timestamp. Our model will have the following fields:

- email (unique): store the user's email address and use that for authentication
- password_hash: instead of stringing each user's password as plaintext, we will hash the password using a one-way cryptographic hash function
- name: the user's name, so we can display it alongside their blog entries
- slug: A URL-friendly representation of the user's name, also unique
- active: Boolean flag indicating whether this account is active. Only active users will be able to log into the site
- created_timestamp: The time this user account was created

> If there are other fields you think might be useful, feel free to make your own additions to this list.

Now that we have our list of fields, let's create the model class. Open models.py and, below the Tag model, add the following code:

```python
class User(db.Model):
    id = db.Column(db.Integer, primary_key=True)
    email = db.Column(db.String(64), unique=True)
    password_hash = db.Column(db.String(255))
    name = db.Column(db.String(64))
    slug = db.Column(db.String(64), unique=True)
    active = db.Column(db.Boolean, default=True)
    created_timestamp = db.Column(db.DateTime, default=datetime.
datetime.now)

    def __init__(self, *args, **kwargs):
        super(User, self).__init__(*args, **kwargs)
        self.generate_slug()

    def generate_slug(self):
        if self.name:
            self.slug = slugify(self.name)
```

As you'll recall from *Chapter 2, Relational Databases with SQLAlchemy*, we need to create a migration in order to add this table to our database. From the command line, we will use the `manage.py` helper to introspect our models and generate the migration script:

```
(blog) $ python manage.py db migrate
INFO   [alembic.migration] Context impl SQLiteImpl.
INFO   [alembic.migration] Will assume non-transactional DDL.
INFO   [alembic.autogenerate.compare] Detected added table 'user'
  Generating /home/charles/projects/blog/app/migrations/
versions/40ce2670e7e2_.py
... done
```

Having generated the migration, we can now run `db upgrade` to make the schema changes:

```
(blog) $ python manage.py db upgrade
INFO   [alembic.migration] Context impl SQLiteImpl.
INFO   [alembic.migration] Will assume non-transactional DDL.
INFO   [alembic.migration] Running upgrade 2ceb72931f66 ->
40ce2670e7e2, empty message
```

Now that we have users, the next step will be to allow them to log into the site.

# Installing Flask-Login

Flask-Login is a lightweight extension that handles logging users in and out of the site. From the project's documentation, Flask-Login will do the following:

- Log users in and out of the site
- Restrict views to the logged-in users
- Manage cookies and the "remember me" functionality
- Help protect user session cookies from being stolen

On the other hand, Flask-Login will not do the following:

- Make any decisions about the storage of user accounts
- Manage usernames, passwords, OpenIDs, or any other form of credentials
- Handle tiered permissions or anything beyond logged in or logged out
- Account registration, activation, or password reminders

The takeaway from these lists is that Flask-Login can best be thought of as a session manager. It simply manages user sessions and lets us know which user is making a request, and whether that user is logged in or not.

Let's get started. Use `pip` to install Flask-Login:

```
(blog) $ pip install Flask-Login
Downloading/unpacking Flask-Login
...
Successfully installed Flask-Login
Cleaning up...
```

In order to start using the extension in our app, we will create an instance of the `LoginManager` class, which is provided by Flask-Login. In addition to creating the `LoginManager` object, we will add a signal handler that will run before every request. This signal handler will retrieve the currently logged-in user and store it on a special object named `g`. In Flask, the `g` object can be used to store arbitrary values per-request.

Add the following lines of code to `app.py`. The imports go at the top of the module, and the rest goes at the end:

```python
from flask import Flask, g
from flask.ext.login import LoginManager, current_user

# Add to the end of the module.
login_manager = LoginManager(app)
login_manager.login_view = "login"

@app.before_request
def _before_request():
    g.user = current_user
```

Now that we have created our `login_manager` and added a signal handler to load the current user, we need to tell Flask-Login how to determine which user is logged in. The way Flask-Login determines this is by storing the current user's ID in the session. Our user loader will accept the ID that was stored in the session and return a `User` object from the database.

Open `models.py` and add the following lines of code:

```python
from app import login_manager

@login_manager.user_loader
def _user_loader(user_id):
    return User.query.get(int(user_id))
```

Now Flask-Login knows how to convert a user ID into a User object, and that user will be available to us as g.user.

# Implementing the Flask-Login interface

In order for Flask-Login to work with our User model, we need to implement a handful of special methods that comprise the Flask-Login interface. By implementing these methods, Flask-Login will be able to take a User object and determine whether they can log into the site.

Open models.py and add the following methods to the User class:

```
class User(db.Model):
    # ... column definitions, etc ...

    # Flask-Login interface..
    def get_id(self):
        return unicode(self.id)

    def is_authenticated(self):
        return True

    def is_active(self):
        return self.active

    def is_anonymous(self):
        return False
```

The first method, get_id(), instructs Flask-Login how to determine the ID of a user, which will then be stored in the session. It is the inverse of our User Loader function, which gives us an ID and asks us to return a User object. The rest of the methods tell Flask-Login that User objects from the database are not anonymous, and should be allowed to login only if the active attribute is set to True. Recall that Flask-Login knows nothing about our User model or our database, so we have to be very explicit in what we tell it.

Now that we have configured Flask-Login, let's add the code that will allow us to create some users.

# Creating user objects

Creating a new user is just like creating an entry or tag with one exception: we need to securely hash the user's password. You should never store passwords as plaintext and, due to the ever-increasing sophistication of hackers, it is best to use a strong cryptographic hash function. We will be using the **Flask-Bcrypt** extension to hash and check our passwords, so let's install the extension using `pip`:

```
(blog) $ pip install flask-bcrypt
...
Successfully installed Flask-Bcrypt
Cleaning up...
```

Open `app.py` and add the following code to register the extension with our app:

```python
from flask.ext.bcrypt import Bcrypt

bcrypt = Bcrypt(app)
```

Now let's add some methods to the `User` object that will make creating and checking passwords straightforward:

```python
from app import bcrypt

class User(db.Model):
    # ... column definitions, other methods ...

    @staticmethod
    def make_password(plaintext):
        return bcrypt.generate_password_hash(plaintext)

    def check_password(self, raw_password):
        return bcrypt.check_password_hash(self.password_hash, raw_
password)

    @classmethod
    def create(cls, email, password, **kwargs):
        return User(
            email=email,
            password_hash=User.make_password(password),
            **kwargs)

    @staticmethod
    def authenticate(email, password):
```

```
user = User.query.filter(User.email == email).first()
if user and user.check_password(password):
    return user
return False
```

The `make_password` method accepts a plaintext password and returns the hashed version, while the `check_password` method accepts a plaintext password and determines whether it matches the hashed version stored in the database. We will not use these methods directly, however. Instead, we will create two higher-level methods, `create` and `authenticate`. The `create` method will create a new user, automatically hashing the password before saving, and the `authenticate` method will retrieve a user given a username and password.

Let's experiment with these methods by creating a new user. Open up a shell and, using the following code as an example, create a user for yourself:

```
In [1]: from models import User, db

In [2]: user = User.create("charlie@gmail.com", password="secret",
name="Charlie")

In [3]: print user.password
$2a$12$q.rRa.6Y2IEF1omVIzkPieWfsNJzpWN6nNofBxuMQDKn.As/8dzoG

In [4]: db.session.add(user)

In [5]: db.session.commit()

In [6]:  User.authenticate("charlie@gmail.com", "secret")
Out[6]:  <User u"Charlie">

In [7]: User.authenticate("charlie@gmail.com", "incorrect")
Out[7]: False
```

Now that we have a way to securely store and verify a user's credentials, we can commence with building the login and logout views.

# Login and logout views

Users will log into our blogging site using their email and password; so, before we begin building our actual login view, let's start with the `LoginForm`. This form will accept the `username`, `password`, and will also present a checkbox to indicate whether the site should `remember me`. Create a `forms.py` module in the `app` directory and add the following code:

```
import wtforms
from wtforms import validators
from models import User

class LoginForm(wtforms.Form):
    email = wtforms.StringField("Email",
        validators=[validators.DataRequired()])
    password = wtforms.PasswordField("Password",
        validators=[validators.DataRequired()])
    remember_me = wtforms.BooleanField("Remember me?",
        default=True)
```

> Note that WTForms also provides an e-mail validator. However, as the documentation for this validator tells us, it is very primitive and may not capture all edge cases as full e-mail validation is actually extremely difficult.

In order to validate the user's credentials as part of the normal WTForms validation process, we will override the form's `validate()` method. In the event the email is not found or the password does not match, we will display an error below the email field. Add the following method to the `LoginForm` class:

```
def validate(self):
    if not super(LoginForm, self).validate():
        return False

    self.user = User.authenticate(self.email.data, self.password.data)
    if not self.user:
        self.email.errors.append("Invalid email or password.")
        return False

    return True
```

Now that our form is ready, let's create the login view. We will instantiate the `LoginForm` and validate it on `POST`. In addition, when the user successfully authenticates, we will redirect them to a new page.

When a user logs in, it is a good practice to redirect them back to the page the user was previously browsing. To accomplish this, we will store the URL for the page the user was previously at in a query string value called `next`. If a URL is found in this value, we can redirect the user there. If no URL is found, the user will get redirected to the homepage by default.

Open `views.py` in the `app` directory and add the following code:

```
from flask import flash, redirect, render_template, request,
url_for
from flask.ext.login import login_user

from app import app
from app import login_manager
from forms import LoginForm

@app.route("/")
def homepage():
    return render_template("homepage.html")

@app.route("/login/", methods=["GET", "POST"])
def login():
    if request.method == "POST":
        form = LoginForm(request.form)
        if form.validate():
            login_user(form.user, remember=form.remember_me.data)
            flash("Successfully logged in as %s." % form.user.email,
"success")
            return redirect(request.args.get("next") or url_
for("homepage"))
    else:
        form = LoginForm()
    return render_template("login.html", form=form)
```

The magic happens on `POST` after we've successfully validated the form (and therefore authenticated the user). We are calling `login_user`, a helper function provided by Flask-Login, which handles setting the correct session values. Then we set a flash message and send the user on their way.

# The login template

The login.html template is straightforward with the exception of one trick, one exception. In the form's action attribute, we are specifying url_for('login') but we are also passing an extra value next. This allows us to preserve the desired next URL while the user is logging in. Add the following code to templates/login.html:

```
{% extends "base.html" %}
{% from "macros/form_field.html" import form_field %}
{% block title %}Log in{% endblock %}
{% block content_title %}Log in{% endblock %}
{% block content %}
<form action="{{ url_for('login', next=request.args.get('next',''))
}}" class="form form-horizontal" method="post">
{{ form_field(form.email) }}
{{ form_field(form.password) }}
<div class="form-group">
    <div class="col-sm-offset-3 col-sm-9">
        <div class="checkbox">
            <label>{{ form.remember_me() }} Remember me</label>
        </div>
    </div>
</div>
<div class="form-group">
    <div class="col-sm-offset-3 col-sm-9">
        <button type="submit" class="btn btn-default">Log in</button>
        <a class="btn" href="{{ url_for('homepage') }}">Cancel</a>
    </div>
</div>
</form>
{% endblock %}
```

When you visit the login page, your form will look something like the following screenshot:

## Logging out

Finally let's add a view for logging users out of the site. Interestingly, no template is needed for this view because users will simply pass through the view, being redirected after their session is logged out. Add the following `import` statement and logout view code to `views.py`:

```
# Modify the import at the top of the module.
from flask.ext.login import login_user, logout_user  # Add
logout_user

@app.route("/logout/")
def logout():
    logout_user()
    flash('You have been logged out.', 'success')
    return redirect(request.args.get('next') or url_for('homepage'))
```

Once again, we are accepting a `next` URL as part of the query string, defaulting to the homepage if no URL is specified.

# Accessing the current user

Let's create links to the login and logout views in the navigation bar. To do this, we will need to check whether the current user is authenticated. If so, we will display a link to the logout view; otherwise, we will display a link to log in.

As you may recall from earlier in the chapter, we added a signal handler that stores the current user as an attribute of the Flask g object. We can access this object in the template, so we simply need to check, in the template, whether g.user is authenticated or not.

Open base.html and make the following additions to the navigation bar:

```html
<ul class="nav navbar-nav">
    <li><a href="{{ url_for('homepage') }}">Home</a></li>
    <li><a href="{{ url_for('entries.index') }}">Blog</a></li>
    {% if g.user.is_authenticated %}
    <li><a href="{{ url_for('logout', next=request.path) }}">Log
out</a></li>
    {% else %}
    <li><a href="{{ url_for('login', next=request.path) }}">Log
in</a></li>
    {% endif %}
  {% block extra_nav %}{% endblock %}
</ul>
```

Note how we are calling the is_authenticated() method, which we implemented on our User model. Flask-Login provides us with a special AnonymousUserMixin that will be used if no user is currently logged in.

Also note that, in addition to the view name, we are specifying next=request.path. This works in tandem with our login and logout views, to redirect the user to their current page after clicking login or logout.

# Restricting access to views

At the moment, all of our blog views are currently unprotected and available to anyone who wants to visit them. In order to prevent a malicious user from trashing our entries, let's add some protection to the views that actually modify data. Flask-Login provides a special decorator login_required that we will use to protect views that should require an authenticated user.

Let's go through the entries blueprint and protect all views that modify data. Start by adding the following import at the top of the blueprint.py module:

```python
from flask.ext.login import login_required
```

login_required is a decorator, just like app.route, so we will simply wrap the views that we wish to protect. For example, this is how you would protect the image_upload view:

```
@entries.route('/image-upload/', methods=['GET', 'POST'])
@login_required
def image_upload():
    ...
```

Go through the module and add the login_required decorator to the following views, taking care to add it below the route decorator:

- image_upload
- create
- edit
- delete

When an anonymous user attempts to access these views, they will be redirected to the login view. As an added bonus, Flask-Login will automatically handle specifying the next parameter when redirecting to the login view, so users will be returned to the page they were attempting to access.

## Storing an entry's author

As you might recall from the spec we created in *Chapter 1, Creating your First Flask Application*, our blogging site will support multiple authors. When an entry is created, we will store the current user in the entry's author column. In order to store the User who authored a given Entry, we will be creating a *one-to-many* relationship between users and entries, such that one user may have many entries:

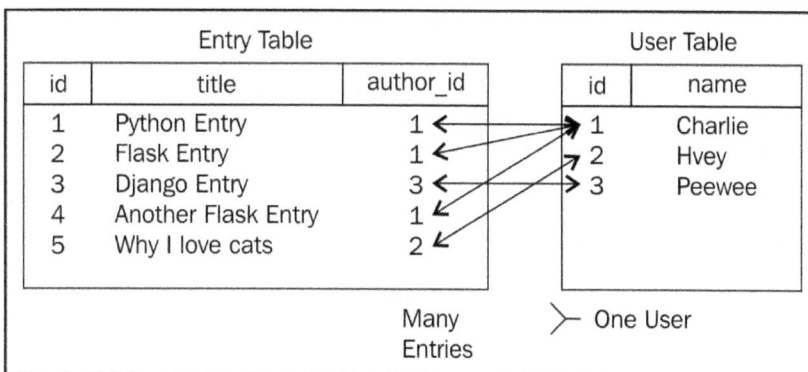

To create a *one-to-many* relationship, we will add a column to the `Entry` model that points to a user in the `User` table. This column will be named `author_id` and, because it references a `User`, we will make this a foreign key. Open `models.py` and make the following modification to the `Entry` model:

```
class Entry(db.Model):
    modified_timestamp = ...
    author_id = db.Column(db.Integer, db.ForeignKey("user.id"))

    tags = ...
```

Since we've added a new column, we once again need to create a migration. From the command line, run `db migrate` and `db upgrade` once more:

```
(blog) $ python manage.py db migrate
INFO  [alembic.migration] Context impl SQLiteImpl.
INFO  [alembic.migration] Will assume non-transactional DDL.
INFO  [alembic.autogenerate.compare] Detected added column
'entry.author_id'
  Generating /home/charles/projects/blog/app/migrations/
versions/33011181124e_.py
... done


(blog) $ python manage.py db upgrade
INFO  [alembic.migration] Context impl SQLiteImpl.
INFO  [alembic.migration] Will assume non-transactional DDL.
INFO  [alembic.migration] Running upgrade 40ce2670e7e2 ->
33011181124e, empty message
```

Like we did with tags, the final step will be to create a back-reference on the User model that will allow us to access a given user's associated `Entry` rows. Because a user may have many entries we would like to perform additional filtering operations on, we will expose the back-reference as a query, just like we did for tag.entries.

In the `User` class, add the following line of code below the `created_timestamp` column:

```
entries = db.relationship('Entry', backref='author', lazy='dynamic')
```

We now have the ability to store a `User` as the author of a blog entry, and the next step will be to populate this column at the time the entry is created.

> If there are any blog entries in the database, we also need to be sure that they are assigned to an author. From the interactive shell, let's manually update the author field on all existing entries:
>
> ```
> In [8]: Entry.query.update({"author_id": user.id})
> Out[8]: 6
> ```
>
> The query will return the number of rows updated, which in this case is the number of entries in the database. To save these changes, once again call commit():
>
> ```
> In [9]: db.session.commit()
> ```

# Setting the author on blog entries

Now that we have a column suitable for storing the author of the Entry, and are able to access the currently logged-in user, we can put that information to use by setting the author of an entry at the time it is created. Before each request, our signal handler will patch the current user onto the Flask g object, and since the create view is protected by the login_required decorator, we know that g.user will be a User from the database.

Because we are using the g object to access the user, we will need to import it, so add the following import statement to the top of the entries blueprint:

```
from flask import g
```

In the entries blueprint, we now need to modify the instantiation of the Entry object to manually set the author attribute. Make the following change to the create view:

```
if form.validate():
    entry = form.save_entry(Entry(author=g.user))
    db.session.add(entry)
```

When you go to create an entry, you will now be saved in the database as the author of that entry. Go ahead and try it out.

# Protecting the edit and delete views

If multiple users are able to log into our site, there's nothing to stop a malicious user from editing or even deleting another user's entries. These views are protected by the login_required decorator, but we need to add some additional code to ensure that only the author can edit or delete their own entries.

In order to implement this protection cleanly, we will once again refactor the helper functions in the entries blueprint. Make the following modifications to the entries blueprint:

```
def get_entry_or_404(slug, author=None):
    query = Entry.query.filter(Entry.slug == slug)
    if author:
        query = query.filter(Entry.author == author)
    else:
        query = filter_status_by_user(query)
    return query.first_or_404()
```

We have introduced a new helper function, `filter_status_by_user`. This function will ensure that anonymous users cannot see draft entries. Add the following function to the entries blueprint below `get_entry_or_404`:

```
def filter_status_by_user(query):
    if not g.user.is_authenticated:
        return query.filter(Entry.status == Entry.STATUS_PUBLIC)
    else:
        return query.filter(
            Entry.status.in_((Entry.STATUS_PUBLIC,
Entry.STATUS_DRAFT)))
```

In order to restrict access to the `edit` and `delete` views, we now only need to pass in the current user as the author parameter. Make the following modification to the edit and delete views:

```
entry = get_entry_or_404(slug, author=None)
```

If you were to attempt to access the `edit` or `delete` view for an entry you did not create, you would receive a `404` response.

Finally, let's modify the entry detail template to hide the *Edit* and *Delete* links from all users except the entry's author. In your `entries` app edit the template `entries/detail.html`, your code might look something like this:

```
{% if g.user == entry.author %}
  <li><h4>Actions</h4></li>
  <li><a href="{{ url_for('entries.edit', slug=entry.slug)
}}">Edit</a></li>
<li><a href="{{ url_for('entries.delete', slug=entry.slug)
}}">Delete</a></li>
{% endif %}
```

# Displaying a user's drafts

There is still one slight problem with our entry list: draft entries are displayed alongside normal entries. We don't want to display unfinished entries to just anyone, but at the same time it would be helpful for a user to see their own drafts. For that reason, we will modify the entry lists and detail to display only public entries to everyone but the author of the entry.

Once again we will be modifying the helper functions in the entries blueprint. We will first modify the `filter_status_by_user` function to allow logged-in users to view their own drafts (but not anyone else's):

```
def filter_status_by_user(query):
    if not g.user.is_authenticated:
        query = query.filter(Entry.status == Entry.STATUS_PUBLIC)
    else:
        # Allow user to view their own drafts.
        query = query.filter(
            (Entry.status == Entry.STATUS_PUBLIC) |
            ((Entry.author == g.user) &
             (Entry.status != Entry.STATUS_DELETED)))
    return query
```

The new query could be parsed as— "Give me all the public entries, or the undeleted entries for which I am the author."

Since `get_entry_or_404` is using the `filter_status_by_user` helper already, the `detail`, `edit`, and `delete` views are ready to go. We only need to address the various list views, which use the `entry_list` helper. Let's update the `entry_list` helper to use the new `filter_status_by_user` helper:

```
    query = filter_status_by_user(query)

    valid_statuses = (Entry.STATUS_PUBLIC, Entry.STATUS_DRAFT)
    query = query.filter(Entry.status.in_(valid_statuses))
    if request.args.get("q"):
        search = request.args["q"]
        query = query.filter(
            (Entry.body.contains(search)) |
            (Entry.title.contains(search)))
    return object_list(template, query, **context)
```

That's all that it takes! I hope this shows how a few helper functions, in the right places, can really simplify your life as a developer. Before continuing on to the final section, I'd suggest creating one or two users and experimenting with the new functionality.

If you plan on supporting multiple authors on your blog, you could also add an authors' index page (like the tag index), and author detail pages that list the entries associated with a given author (`user.entries`).

# Sessions

As you've worked through this chapter, you may have wondered how Flask-Login (and also Flask) are able to determine which user is logged in between requests, request after request. Flask-Login does this by storing a user's ID in a special object called the session. Sessions utilize cookies to securely store morsels of information. When the user makes a request to your Flask application, their cookies are sent along with the request, and Flask is able to inspect the cookie data and load it into the session object. Similarly, your views can add or modify information stored in the session, updating the user's cookies in the process.

The beauty of Flask's session object is that it can be used for any visitor to the site, whether they are logged in or not. The session can be treated just like an ordinary Python dictionary. The following code shows how you might track the last page a user visited using the session:

```
from flask import request, session

@app.before_request
def _last_page_visited():
    if "current_page" in session:
        session["last_page"] = session["current_page"]
    session["current_page"] = request.path
```

By default, Flask sessions last only as long as the browser is open. If you would like the session to persist, even between restarts, simply set `session.permanent = True`.

> Like the g object, the `session` object can be accessed directly from the template.

As an exercise, try implementing a simple theme chooser for your website. Create a view that allows users to pick a color theme, which will be stored in the session. Then, in the templates, apply extra CSS rules depending on the user's chosen theme.

# Summary

In this chapter, we added user authentication to the blogging app. We created a User model, which securely stores a user's login credentials in the database, then built views for logging users in and out of the site. We added a signal handler that runs before every request and retrieves the current user, then learned how to use this information in the views and templates. In the second half of the chapter, we integrated the User model with the Entry model, making our blog more secure in the process. The chapter wrapped up with a brief discussion of Flask sessions.

In the next chapter, we will build an administrative dashboard that will allow super-users to perform actions such as creating new users and modifying site content. We will also collect and display various site metrics, such as page-views, to help visualize what content is driving the most traffic.

# 6
# Building an Administrative Dashboard

In this chapter, we will build an administrative dashboard for our website. Our admin dashboard will give certain, selected, users the ability to manage all the content across the entire site. In essence, the admin site will be a graphical frontend for the database, supporting operations for creating, editing, and deleting rows in our application's tables. The excellent Flask-Admin extension provides almost all these functionalities out-of-the- box, but we will go beyond the defaults to extend and customize the admin pages.

In this chapter we shall:

- Install Flask-Admin and add it to our website
- Add views for working with the `Entry`, `Tag`, and `User` models
- Add a view for managing the website's static assets
- Integrate the admin with the Flask-Login framework
- Create a column to identify a user as an administrator
- Create a custom index page for the admin dashboard

## Installing Flask-Admin

Flask-Admin provides a readymade admin interface for Flask applications. Flask-Admin also integrates nicely with SQLAlchemy to provide views for managing your application's models.

The following image gives is a sneak preview of what the **Entry** admin will look like by the end of this chapter:

| | | Title | Status | Author | Tease | Tag List | Created Timestamp |
|---|---|---|---|---|---|---|---|
| ☐ | ✏ 🗑 | Python Entry | 0 | <User u'Charlie'> | This is an entry about Python, my favorite programming language. | python | 2014-03-06 19:50:09.799768 |
| ☐ | ✏ 🗑 | Flask entry | 0 | <User u'Charlie'> | This is an entry about Flask, my favorite python framework. | python, flask | 2014-03-06 19:50:26.948381 |
| ☐ | ✏ 🗑 | Django entry | 0 | <User u'Charlie'> | This is an entry about Django, the first web framework I learned to use. | django, python | 2014-03-06 19:51:43.889176 |
| ☐ | ✏ 🗑 | My draft | 1 | <User u'Charlie'> | This is a draft post I'm working on. | | 2014-03-06 19:52:06.102482 |
| ☐ | ✏ 🗑 | Huey's first post | 0 | <User u'Huey'> | This is Huey's first post. | Kittens, Cats | 2014-03-06 19:53:26.302281 |
| ☐ | ✏ 🗑 | Huey's work in progress | 1 | <User u'Huey'> | This is one of Huey's drafts. | | 2014-03-06 19:53:40.272277 |

(Blog Admin — Home, Entry, Tag, User, Static Files — List (6), Create, Add Filter, With selected, Search)

While this amount of functionality requires relatively little code, we still have a lot to cover, so let's get started. Begin by installing `Flask-Admin` into `virtualenv` using `pip`. At the time of writing, the current version of Flask-Admin is 1.0.7.

```
(blog) $ pip install Flask-Admin
Downloading/unpacking Flask-Admin
...
Successfully installed Flask-Admin
Cleaning up...
```

You can test that it installed correctly if you wish by entering the following code:

```
(blog) $ python manage.py shell
In [1]: from flask.ext import admin
In [2]: print admin.__version__
1.0.7
```

# Adding Flask-Admin to our app

Unlike the other extensions in our app, which we instantiated in the app module, we will be setting up the admin extension in its own module. We will be writing several admin-specific classes, so it makes sense to put them in their own module. Create a new module named admin.py in the app directory, and add the following code:

```
from flask.ext.admin import Admin
from app import app

admin = Admin(app, 'Blog Admin')
```

Because our admin module depends on the app module, in order to avoid a circular import we need to be sure that admin is loaded *after* app. Open the main.py module and add the following:

```
from flask import request, session

from app import app, db
import admin  # This line is new, placed after the app import.
import models
import views
```

You should now be able to start the development server and navigate to /admin/ to view a barebones admin–the default dashboard, as seen in the following image:

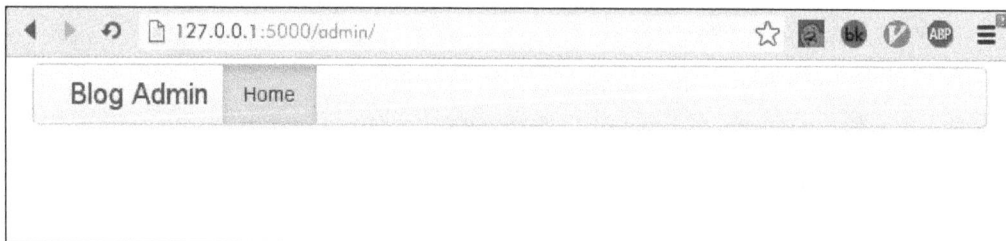

As you progress through this chapter, we will turn this boring and plain admin interface into a rich and powerful dashboard for managing your blog.

# Exposing models through the Admin

Flask-Admin comes with a `contrib` package that contains special view classes designed to work with SQLAlchemy models. These classes provide out-of-the-box create, read, update, and delete functionalities.

Open `admin.py` and update the following code:

```
from flask.ext.admin import Admin
from flask.ext.admin.contrib.sqla import ModelView

from app import app, db
from models import Entry, Tag, User

admin = Admin(app, 'Blog Admin')
admin.add_view(ModelView(Entry, db.session))
admin.add_view(ModelView(Tag, db.session))
admin.add_view(ModelView(User, db.session))
```

Note how we call `admin.add_view()` and pass instances of the `ModelView` class, as well as the `db` session, for it to access the database with. Flask-Admin works by providing a central endpoint to which we, the developers, can then add our own views.

Start the development server and try pulling up your admin site again. It should look something like the following screenshot:

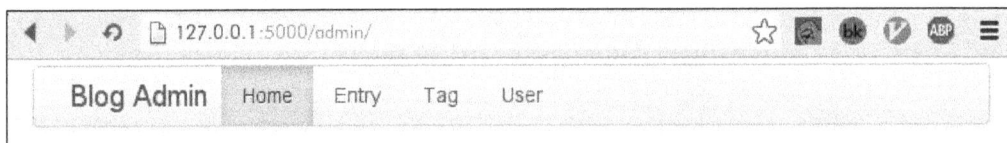

Try clicking into one of our model's views by selecting its link in the navigation bar. Clicking the **Entry** link displays all the entries in the database in a clean, tabular format. There are even links to create, edit, or delete entries as seen in the next screenshot:

| | | Title | Slug | Body | Status | Created Timestamp | Modified Timestamp | Author |
|---|---|---|---|---|---|---|---|---|
| | ✏ 🗑 | Python Entry | python-entry | This is an entry about Python, my favorite programming language. | 0 | 2014-03-06 19:50:09.799768 | 2014-03-06 19:50:09.799807 | <User u'Charlie'> |
| | ✏ 🗑 | Flask entry | flask-entry | This is an entry about Flask, my favorite python framework. | 0 | 2014-03-06 19:50:26.948381 | 2014-03-06 19:50:26.948406 | <User u'Charlie'> |
| | ✏ 🗑 | Django entry | django-entry | This is an entry about Django, the first web framework I learned to use. | 0 | 2014-03-06 19:51:43.889176 | 2014-03-06 19:51:43.889212 | <User u'Charlie'> |

**Blog Admin**  Home  Entry  Tag  User

List (6)  Create  With selected ▾

The defaults provided by Flask-Admin are great, but if you start exploring the interface you will start to notice subtle things that could be improved or cleaned up. For example, it's probably not necessary to include the Entry's body text as a column. Similarly, the **Status** column is displaying the status as an integer, but we would prefer to see the name associated with that integer. We can also click the *Pencil* icon in each of the `Entry` rows. This will take you to the default edit form view that you can use to modify that entry.

It all looks something like the following screenshot:

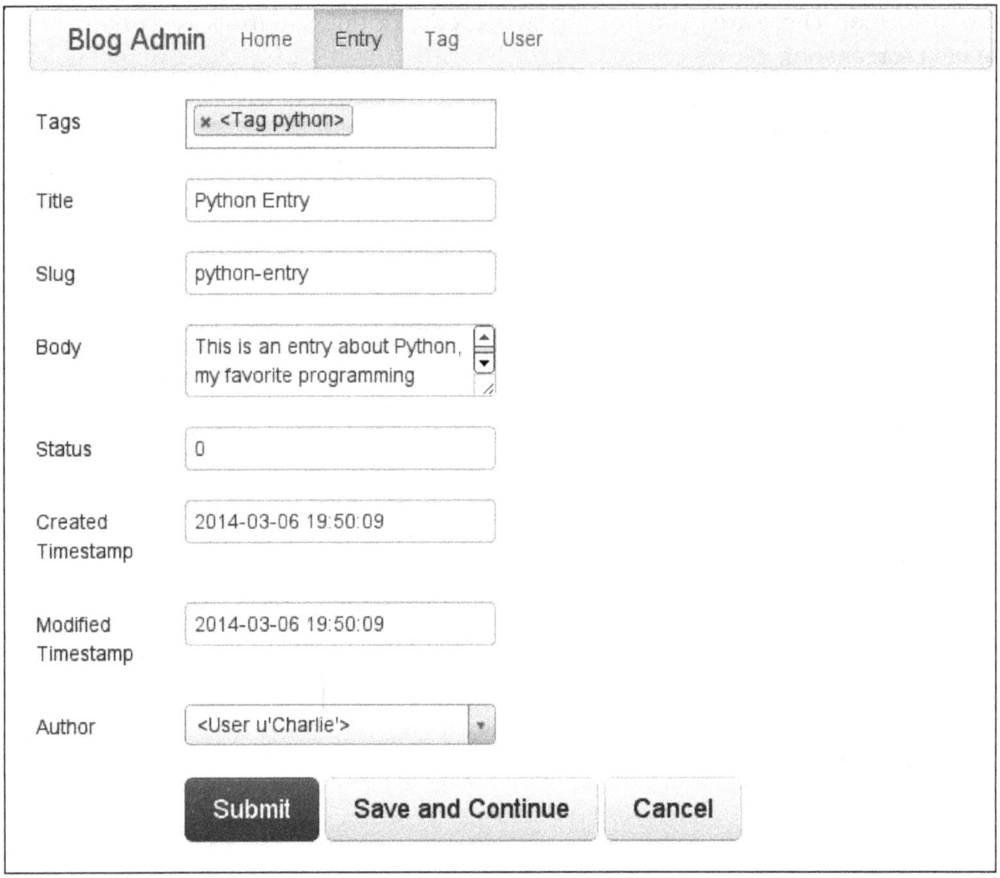

As you can see in the preceding screenshot, Flask-Admin does an impressive job of handling our foreign key-to-key and many-to-many fields (author and tags). It also does a pretty good job choosing which HTML widget to use for a given field as follows:

- Tags can be added and removed using a nice multi-select widget
- Author can be selected using a drop-down menu
- The entry body is conveniently presented as a text area

Unfortunately, there are some obvious problems with this form, as follows:

- The ordering of the fields seems arbitrary.

- The **Slug** field appears as an editable text input since this is managed by the database model. This field should, instead, be generated automatically from the Entry's title.

- The **Status** field is a free-form text input field, but should be a drop-down menu with human-readable status labels rather than numbers.

- The **Created Timestamp** and **Modified Timestamp** fields appear editable, but should be generated automatically.

In the following section, we'll see how to customize the Admin class and the ModelView class, so that the admin really works for our app.

# Customizing the list views

Let's set aside the forms for a moment and focus on cleaning up the list. To do this, we will create a subclass of the Flask-Admin, ModelView. The ModelView class provides numerous extension points and attributes that control the look and feel of the list display.

We'll start by cleaning up the list columns by manually specifying the attributes we wish to display. Additionally, since we are going to be displaying the author in its own column, we will ask Flask-Admin to efficiently fetch it from the database. Open admin.py and update the following code:

```
from flask.ext.admin import Admin
from flask.ext.admin.contrib.sqla import ModelView

from app import app, db
from models import Entry, Tag, User

class EntryModelView(ModelView):
    column_list = [
        'title', 'status', 'author', 'tease', 'tag_list',
'created_timestamp',
    ]
    column_select_related_list = ['author']  # Efficiently SELECT
the author.

admin = Admin(app, 'Blog Admin')
admin.add_view(EntryModelView(Entry, db.session))
admin.add_view(ModelView(Tag, db.session))
admin.add_view(ModelView(User, db.session))
```

You may notice that `tease` and `tag_list` are not actually the names of columns in our `Entry` model. Flask-Admin gives you the ability to use any attribute as a column value. We also specify the column to use for creating references to other models. Open the `models.py` module and add the following properties to the `Entry` model:

```
@property
def tag_list(self):
    return ', '.join(tag.name for tag in self.tags)

@property
def tease(self):
    return self.body[:100]
```

Now, when you visit the **Entry** admin, you should be presented with a clean, readable table as seen in the following image:

| | | Title | Status | Author | Tease | Tag List | Created Timestamp |
|---|---|---|---|---|---|---|---|
| ☐ | ✏ 🗑 | Python Entry | 0 | <User u'Charlie'> | This is an entry about Python, my favorite programming language. | python | 2014-03-06 19:50:09 |
| ☐ | ✏ 🗑 | Flask entry | 0 | <User u'Charlie'> | This is an entry about Flask, my favorite python framework. | python, flask | 2014-03-06 19:50:26.948381 |
| ☐ | ✏ 🗑 | Django entry | 0 | <User u'Charlie'> | This is an entry about Django, the first web framework I learned to use. | django, python | 2014-03-06 19:51:43.889176 |
| ☐ | ✏ 🗑 | My draft | 1 | <User u'Charlie'> | This is a draft post I'm working on. | | 2014-03-06 19:52:06.102482 |

**Blog Admin**  Home  Entry  Tag  User

List (6)  Create  With selected ▾

Let's also fix the display of the **Status** column. Those numbers are difficult to remember – it would be preferable to display a human-readable value. Flask-Admin comes with a helper for *enumerated* fields (such as **Status**). We simply need to provide a mapping of the status value to display the value, and Flask-Admin does the rest. Make the following additions to the `EntryModelView`:

```
class EntryModelView(ModelView):
    _status_choices = [(choice, label) for choice, label in [
        (Entry.STATUS_PUBLIC, 'Public'),
        (Entry.STATUS_DRAFT, 'Draft'),
        (Entry.STATUS_DELETED, 'Deleted'),
    ]]

    column_choices = {
        'status': _status_choices,
    }
    column_list = [
        'title', 'status', 'author', 'tease', 'tag_list',
'created_timestamp',
    ]
    column_select_related_list = ['author']
```

Our `Entry` list view is looking much better. Let's make some improvements
to the `User` list view now. Again, we will subclass `ModelView` and specify the
attributes that we wish to override. Add the following class to `admin.py` below
`EntryModelView`:

```
class UserModelView(ModelView):
    column_list = ['email', 'name', 'active', 'created_timestamp']

# Be sure to use the UserModelView class when registering the
User:
admin.add_view(UserModelView(User, db.session))
```

The following screenshot shows how the `User` list view looks with our changes:

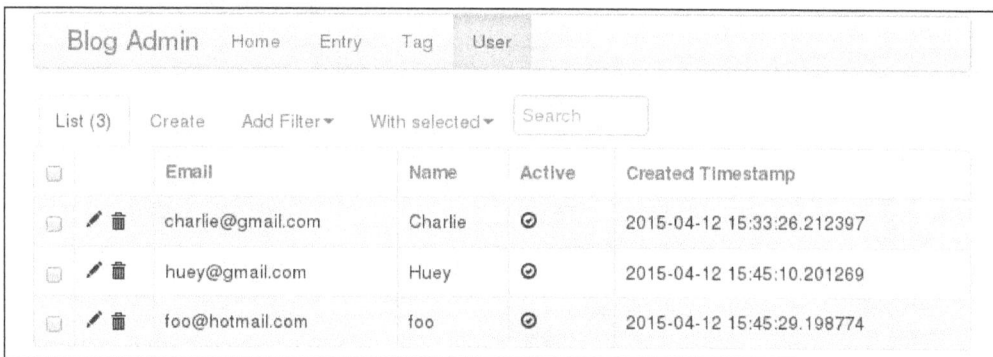

| | | Email | Name | Active | Created Timestamp |
|---|---|---|---|---|---|
| | | charlie@gmail.com | Charlie | ⊘ | 2015-04-12 15:33:26.212397 |
| | | huey@gmail.com | Huey | ⊘ | 2015-04-12 15:45:10.201269 |
| | | foo@hotmail.com | foo | ⊘ | 2015-04-12 15:45:29.198774 |

# Adding search and filtering to the list view

In addition to displaying lists of our model instances, Flask-Admin comes with powerful search and filtering capabilities. Let's suppose we have a large number of entries and want to find those that contain a certain keyword, such as Python. It would be beneficial if, from the list view, we could enter our search and have Flask-Admin list only those entries that contain the word 'Python' in the title or the body.

As you might expect, this is very easy to accomplish. Open `admin.py` and add the following line:

```
class EntryModelView(ModelView):
    _status_choices = [(choice, label) for choice, label in [
        (Entry.STATUS_PUBLIC, 'Public'),
        (Entry.STATUS_DRAFT, 'Draft'),
        (Entry.STATUS_DELETED, 'Deleted'),
    ]]

    column_choices = {
        'status': _status_choices,
    }
    column_list = [
        'title', 'status', 'author', 'tease', 'tag_list',
    'created_timestamp',
    ]
    column_searchable_list = ['title', 'body']
    column_select_related_list = ['author']
```

When you re-load the `Entry` list view, you will see a new textbox that will allow you to search the `title` and `body` fields as seen in the following screenshot:

| | | Title | Status | Author | Tease | Tag List | Created Timestamp |
|---|---|---|---|---|---|---|---|
| ☐ | ✏ 🗑 | Python Entry | Public | <User u'Charlie'> | This is an entry about Python, my favorite programming language. | python | 2014-03-06 19:50:09 |
| ☐ | ✏ 🗑 | Flask entry | Public | <User u'Charlie'> | This is an entry about Flask, my favorite python framework. | python, flask | 2014-03-06 19:50:26.948381 |

List (2)   Create   With selected ▾   Python   ✖

As useful as a full-text search can be, for non-textual fields such as **Status** or **Created Timestamp**, it would be nice to have more powerful filtering capabilities. Again, Flask-Admin comes to the rescue, providing easy-to-use, easy-to-configure filtering options.

Let's see how filters work by adding several to the `Entry` list. Once again, we will be modifying the `EntryModelView` as follows:

```
class EntryModelView(ModelView):
    _status_choices = [(choice, label) for choice, label in [
        (Entry.STATUS_PUBLIC, 'Public'),
        (Entry.STATUS_DRAFT, 'Draft'),
        (Entry.STATUS_DELETED, 'Deleted'),
    ]]

    column_choices = {
        'status': _status_choices,
    }
    column_filters = [
        'status', User.name, User.email, 'created_timestamp'
    ]
    column_list = [
        'title', 'status', 'author', 'tease', 'tag_list',
'created_timestamp',
    ]
    column_searchable_list = ['title', 'body']
    column_select_related_list = ['author']
```

The `column_filters` attribute contains a mixture of the names of columns on the `Entry` model, as well as fields on *related* models such as from `User`:

```
column_filters = [
    'status', User.name, User.email, 'created_timestamp'
]
```

When you access the `Entry` list view, you will now see a new drop-down menu labeled **Add Filter**. Experiment with the various data types. Note that, when you attempt to filter on the **Status** column, Flask-Admin automatically uses the `Public`, `Draft`, and `Deleted` labels. Also note that, when you filter on the **Created Timestamp**, Flask-Admin presents a nice date/time picker widget. In the following screenshot, I've set up a variety of filters:

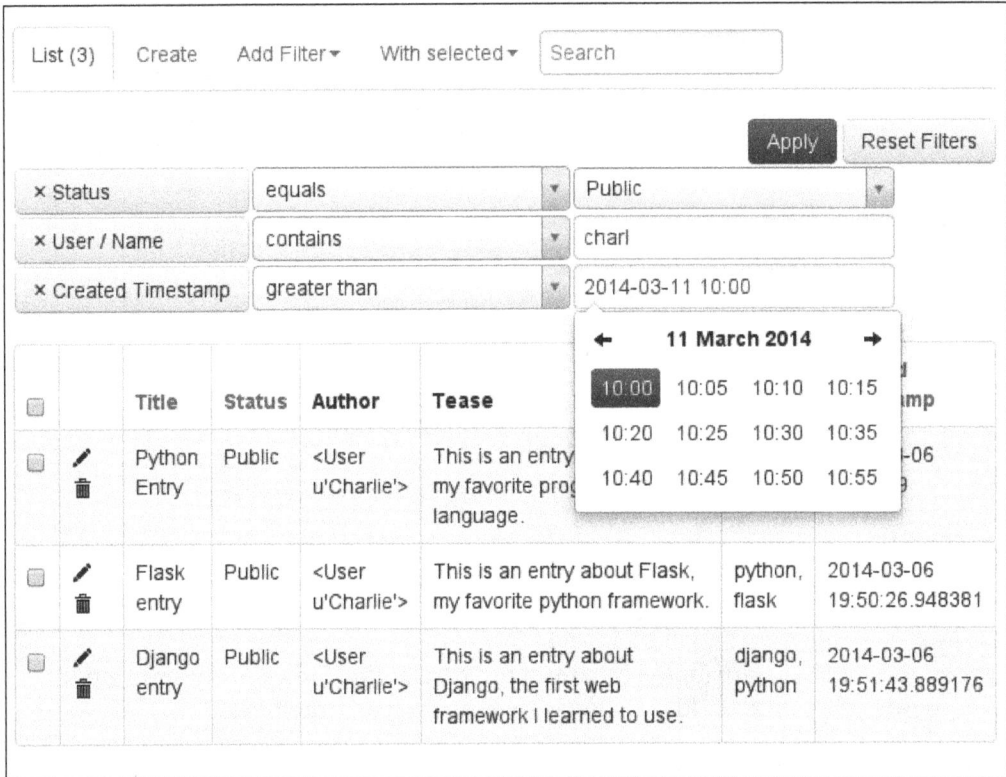

At this point, the `Entry` list view is very functional. As an exercise, set up the `column_filters` and `column_searchable_list` attributes for the `User ModelView`.

# Customizing Admin model forms

We will wrap up the discussion of model views by showing how to customize the form class. As you will recall, there were several limitations with the default forms provided by Flask-Admin. We will show in this section how to customize the display of the form fields used for creating and editing model instances.

Our goal will be to remove the superfluous fields, and to use a more appropriate widget for the **Status** field, achieving what is seen in the following screenshot:

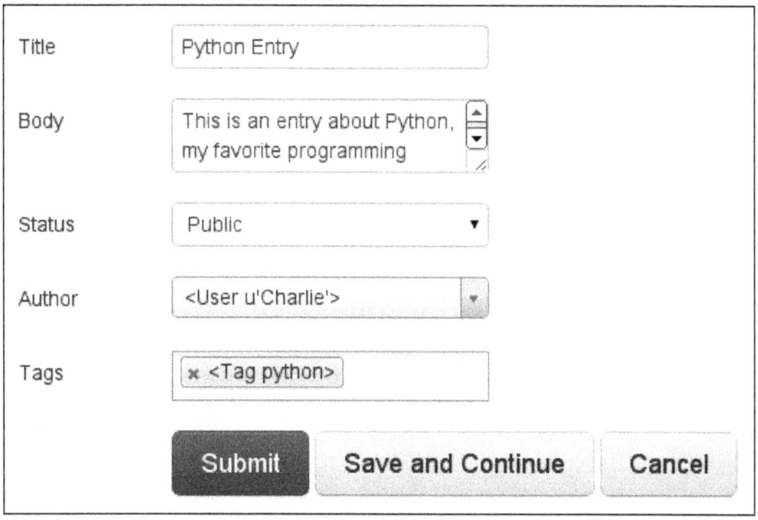

In order to achieve this, we will first manually specify the list of fields that we wish to display on the form. This is done by specifying a `form_columns` attribute on the `EntryModelView` class:

```
class EntryModelView(ModelView):
    ...
    form_columns = ['title', 'body', 'status', 'author', 'tags']
```

Additionally, we wish the `status` field to be a drop-down widget using human-readable labels for the various states. Since we already have defined the status choices, we will instruct Flask-Admin to override the `status` field with a WTForms `SelectField`, and pass in the list of valid choices:

```
from wtforms.fields import SelectField  # At top of module.

class EntryModelView(ModelView):
    ...
    form_args = {
        'status': {'choices': _status_choices, 'coerce': int},
    }
    form_columns = ['title', 'body', 'status', 'author', 'tags']
    form_overrides = {'status': SelectField}
```

By default, the user field will be displayed as a drop-down with simple type ahead. Imagine, though, if this list contained thousands of users! That would result in a very large query and a slow rendering time, due to all the `<option>` elements that would need to be created.

When a form containing a foreign key is rendered to a very large table, Flask-Admin allows us to use Ajax to fetch the desired row. Add the following attribute to the `EntryModelView`, and now your users will be loaded efficiently using Ajax:

```
form_ajax_refs = {
    'author': {
        'fields': (User.name, User.email),
    },
}
```

This directive tells Flask-Admin that, when we are looking up the **Author**, it should allow us to search on the author's name or e-mail. The following screenshot shows what it looks like:

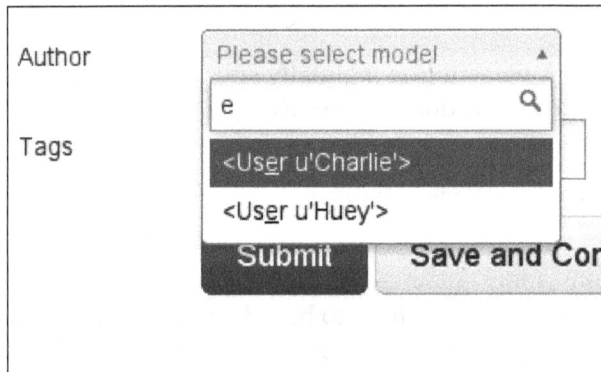

We now have a very nice looking `Entry` form.

# Enhancing the User form

Because passwords are stored as hashes in the database, there is little value in displaying or editing them directly. On the `User` form, however, we will make it possible to enter a new password, replacing the old one. Like we did with the `status` field on the `Entry` form, we will specify a form-field override. Then, in the model change handler, we will update the user's password on-save.

Make the following additions to the `UserModelView` module:

```
from wtforms.fields import PasswordField  # At top of module.

class UserModelView(ModelView):
    column_filters = ('email', 'name', 'active')
    column_list = ['email', 'name', 'active', 'created_timestamp']
    column_searchable_list = ['email', 'name']

    form_columns = ['email', 'password', 'name', 'active']
    form_extra_fields = {
        'password': PasswordField('New password'),
    }

    def on_model_change(self, form, model, is_created):
        if form.password.data:
            model.password_hash =
    User.make_password(form.password.data)
        return super(UserModelView, self).on_model_change(
            form, model, is_created)
```

The following screenshot shows what the new `User` form looks like now. If you wish to change a user's password, simply enter the new one in the **New password** field.

| | |
|---|---|
| Email | huey@gmail.com |
| New password | |
| Name | Huey |
| Active | ☑ |
| Admin | ☐ |

**Submit**    **Save and Continue**    **Cancel**

# Generating slugs

There is still one aspect that we need to address. When creating new `Entry`, `User` or `Tag` objects, Flask-Admin will not correctly generate `slug` for them. This is due to the way Flask-Admin instantiates new model instances when saving. To remedy this, we will create some subclasses of `ModelView` that will ensure that `slug` is generated correctly for `Entry`, `User`, and `Tag` objects

Open `admin.py` and, at the top of the module, add the following classes:

```python
class BaseModelView(ModelView):
    pass


class SlugModelView(BaseModelView):
    def on_model_change(self, form, model, is_created):
        model.generate_slug()
        return super(SlugModelView, self).on_model_change(
            form, model, is_created)
```

These changes instruct Flask-Admin that, whenever a model is changed, slug should be re-generated.

In order to start using this functionality, update the `EntryModelView` and `UserModelView` modules to extend the `SlugModelView` class. For the `Tag` model, it is sufficient to simply register it directly with the `SlugModelView` class.

To summarize, your code should look like the following:

```python
from flask.ext.admin import Admin
from flask.ext.admin.contrib.sqla import ModelView
from wtforms.fields import SelectField

from app import app, db
from models import Entry, Tag, User, entry_tags

class BaseModelView(ModelView):
    pass


class SlugModelView(BaseModelView):
    def on_model_change(self, form, model, is_created):
        model.generate_slug()
        return super(SlugModelView, self).on_model_change(
            form, model, is_created)


class EntryModelView(SlugModelView):
```

```python
    _status_choices = [(choice, label) for choice, label in [
        (Entry.STATUS_PUBLIC, 'Public'),
        (Entry.STATUS_DRAFT, 'Draft'),
        (Entry.STATUS_DELETED, 'Deleted'),
    ]]

    column_choices = {
        'status': _status_choices,
    }
    column_filters = ['status', User.name, User.email,
'created_timestamp']
    column_list = [
        'title', 'status', 'author', 'tease', 'tag_list',
'created_timestamp',
    ]
    column_searchable_list = ['title', 'body']
    column_select_related_list = ['author']

    form_ajax_refs = {
        'author': {
            'fields': (User.name, User.email),
        },
    }
    form_args = {
        'status': {'choices': _status_choices, 'coerce': int},
    }
    form_columns = ['title', 'body', 'status', 'author', 'tags']
    form_overrides = {'status': SelectField}

class UserModelView(SlugModelView):
    column_filters = ('email', 'name', 'active')
    column_list = ['email', 'name', 'active', 'created_timestamp']
    column_searchable_list = ['email', 'name']

    form_columns = ['email', 'password', 'name', 'active']
    form_extra_fields = {
        'password': PasswordField('New password'),
    }

    def on_model_change(self, form, model, is_created):
        if form.password.data:
            model.password_hash =
User.make_password(form.password.data)
```

```
            return super(UserModelView, self).on_model_change(
                form, model, is_created)

    admin = Admin(app, 'Blog Admin')
    admin.add_view(EntryModelView(Entry, db.session))
    admin.add_view(SlugModelView(Tag, db.session))
    admin.add_view(UserModelView(User, db.session))
```

These changes ensure that slugs are generated correctly, whether saving existing objects or creating new ones.

# Managing static assets via the Admin

Flask-Admin provides a convenient interface for managing static assets (or other files on disk) as an extension to the admin dashboard. Let's add a `FileAdmin` to our site that will allow us to upload or modify files in our application's `static` directory.

Open `admin.py` and import the following module at the top of the file:

```
from flask.ext.admin.contrib.fileadmin import FileAdmin
```

Then, below the various `ModelView` implementations, add the following highlighted lines of code:

```
class BlogFileAdmin(FileAdmin):
    pass

admin = Admin(app, 'Blog Admin')
admin.add_view(EntryModelView(Entry, db.session))
admin.add_view(SlugModelView(Tag, db.session))
admin.add_view(UserModelView(User, db.session))
admin.add_view(
    BlogFileAdmin(app.config['STATIC_DIR'], '/static/', name='Static
Files'))
```

Pulling up the admin in your browser, you should see a new tab labeled **Static Files**. Clicking this link will take you to a familiar file-browser, as seen in the following screenshot:

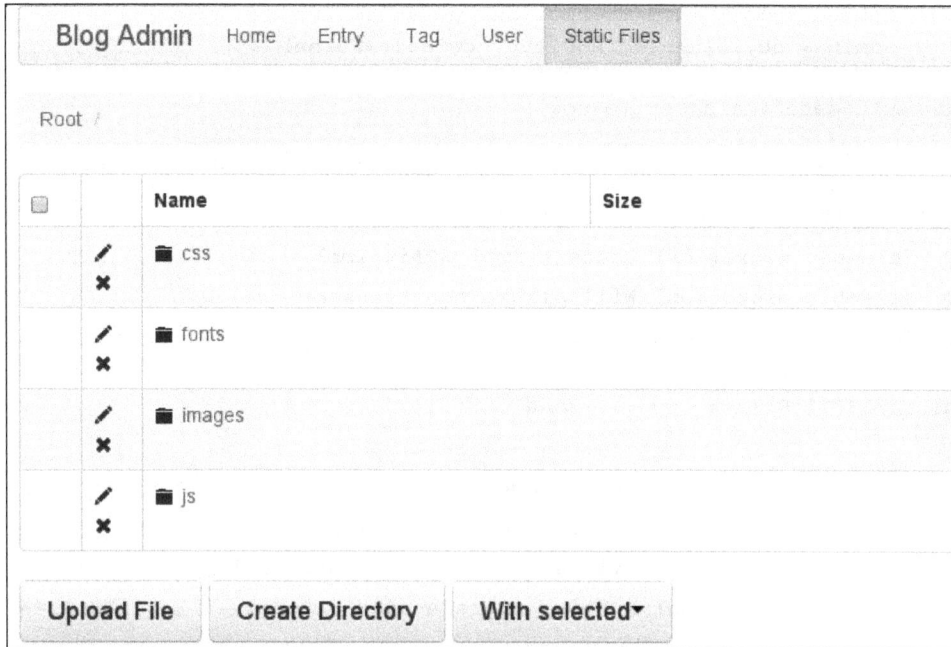

> If you run into issues managing your files, make sure that you have the correct permissions set up for the `static` directory and its children.

# Securing the admin website

As you may have noticed while testing the new admin website, it does not do any sort of authentication. In order to protect our admin site from anonymous users (or even certain logged-in users), we will add a new column to the `User` model to indicate that a user can access the admin website. Then we will use a hook provided by Flask-Admin to ensure that the requesting user has permissions.

The first step is to add a new column to our `User` model. Add the `admin` column to the `User` model as follows:

```
class User(db.Model):
    id = db.Column(db.Integer, primary_key=True)
```

```
        email = db.Column(db.String(64), unique=True)
        password_hash = db.Column(db.String(255))
        name = db.Column(db.String(64))
        slug = db.Column(db.String(64), unique=True)
        active = db.Column(db.Boolean, default=True)
        admin = db.Column(db.Boolean, default=False)
        created_timestamp = db.Column(db.DateTime,
    default=datetime.datetime.now)
```

Now we will generate a schema migration using the Flask-Migrate extension:

```
(blog) $ python manage.py db migrate
INFO   [alembic.migration] Context impl SQLiteImpl.
INFO   [alembic.migration] Will assume non-transactional DDL.
INFO   [alembic.autogenerate.compare] Detected added column 'user.admin'
  Generating /home/charles/projects/blog/app/migrations/
versions/33011181124e_.py ... done


(blog) $ python manage.py db upgrade
INFO   [alembic.migration] Context impl SQLiteImpl.
INFO   [alembic.migration] Will assume non-transactional DDL.
INFO   [alembic.migration] Running upgrade 40ce2670e7e2 -> 33011181124e,
empty message
```

Let's also add a method to the User model that will tell us if the given user is an admin. Add the following method to the User model:

```
    class User(db.Model):
        # ...

        def is_admin(self):
            return self.admin
```

This may seem silly, but it's good code-hygiene should you ever wish to change the semantics of how your app determines whether a user is an admin.

Before continuing on to the next section, you may want to modify the UserModelView class to include the admin column in column_list, column_filters, and form_columns.

# Creating an authentication and authorization mixin

Since we have created several views in our admin view, we need a reusable way of expressing our authentication logic. We will achieve this reuse through composition. You've seen composition already in the form of view decorators (`@login_required`) – decorators are just a way of composing multiple functions. Flask-Admin is a little different in that it uses Python classes to represent an individual view. Instead of function decorators, we will use a class-friendly method of composition called **mixins**.

A mixin is a class that provides a method override. In the case of Flask-Admin, the method we wish to override is the `is_accessible` method. Inside this method, we will check whether the current user is authenticated.

In order to access the current user, we must import the special `g` object at the top of the `admin` module:

```
from flask import g, url_for
```

Below the import statements, add the following class:

```
class AdminAuthentication(object):
    def is_accessible(self):
        return g.user.is_authenticated and g.user.is_admin()
```

Finally, we will be *mixing* it in with several other classes through Python's multiple inheritances. Make the following changes to the `BaseModelView` class:

```
class BaseModelView(AdminAuthentication, ModelView):
    pass
```

And also to the `BlogFileAdmin` class:

```
class BlogFileAdmin(AdminAuthentication, FileAdmin):
    pass
```

If you attempt to access an admin view URL such as /admin/entry/ without meeting the `is_accessible` criteria, Flask-Admin will return an HTTP 403 Forbidden response as seen in the following screenshot:

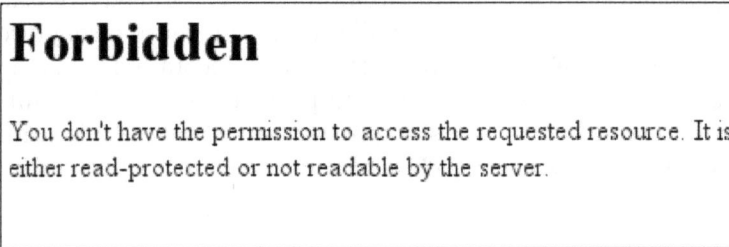

# Forbidden

You don't have the permission to access the requested resource. It is either read-protected or not readable by the server.

> As we have not made changes to the `Tag` admin model this is still accessible. We will leave it up to you to work out how to protect it.

# Setting up a custom index page

The landing page for our admin (/admin/) is very boring. In fact, it has no content at all besides a navigation bar. Flask-Admin allows us to specify a custom index view, which we will use to display a simple greeting.

In order to add a custom index view, we need to import several new helpers. Add the following highlighted imports to the top of the `admin` module:

```
from flask.ext.admin import Admin, AdminIndexView, expose
```

`from flask import redirect` request provides the `@expose` decorator much like Flask itself uses `@route`. Since this view is the index, the URL we will be exposing is /. The following code will create a simple index view that renders a template. Note that we specify the index view as a parameter when initializing the `Admin` object:

```
class IndexView(AdminIndexView):
    @expose('/')
    def index(self):
        return self.render('admin/index.html')


admin = Admin(app, 'Blog Admin', index_view=IndexView())
```

One final piece is missing: authentication. Since users will commonly access the admin by going directly to /admin/, it would be handy to redirect unauthenticated users to a login page. We can do that by checking, in the index view, whether the current user is authenticated as follows:

```
class IndexView(AdminIndexView):
    @expose('/')
    def index(self):
        if not (g.user.is_authenticated and g.user.is_admin()):
            return redirect(url_for('login', next=request.path))
        return self.render('admin/index.html')
```

# Flask-Admin templates

Flask-Admin provides a simple master template that you can extend to create a uniform look to your admin site. The Flask-Admin master template comprises the following blocks:

| Block Name | Description |
|---|---|
| head_meta | Page metadata in header |
| title | Page title |
| head_css | CSS links in header |
| head | Arbitrary content in document header |
| page_body | Page layout |
| brand | Logo in the menu bar |
| main_menu | Main menu |
| menu_links | Navigation bar |
| access_control | Section to the right of the menu that can be used to add login/logout buttons |
| messages | Alerts and various messages |
| body | Main content area |
| tail | Empty area below content |

The body block will be of most interest to us for this example. In your application's templates directory, create a new sub-directory named admin containing a blank file named index.html.

Let's customize the admin landing page to display the current date and time on the server. We will extend the master template provided by Flask-Admin, overriding just the body block. Create the admin directory in templates and add the following code to templates/admin/index.html:

```
{% extends "admin/master.html" %}

{% block body %}
  <h3>Hello, {{ g.user.name }}</h3>
{% endblock %}
```

The following is a screenshot of our new landing page:

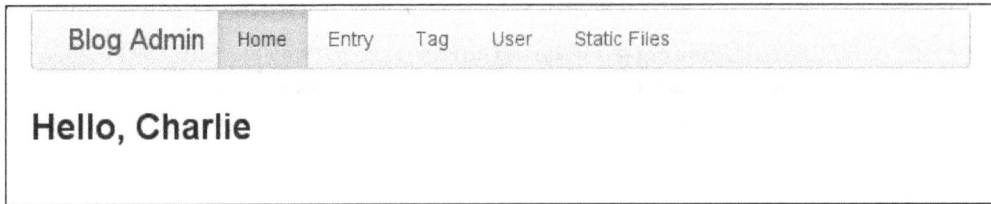

| Blog Admin | Home | Entry | Tag | User | Static Files |

**Hello, Charlie**

This is just an example to illustrate how simple it is to extend and customize your admin dashboard. Experiment with the various template blocks, and see if you can add a logout button to the navigation bar.

# Reading more

Flask-Admin is a versatile, highly-configurable Flask extension. While we covered a number of the more commonly-used features of Flask-Admin, there are simply too many features to discuss in a single chapter. So, I strongly suggest that you visit the project's documentation if you would like to continue learning. The documentation can be found online at `https://flask-admin.readthedocs.org/`.

# Summary

In this chapter, we learned how to create an administrative dashboard for our app using the Flask-Admin extension. We learned how to expose our SQLAlchemy models as lists of editable objects, as well as how to customize the look and feel of the tables and the forms. We added a file-browser to assist in managing our app's static assets. We also integrated the admin with our authentication system.

In the next chapter, we will learn about adding APIs to our application so that we can access it programmatically.

# 7
# AJAX and RESTful APIs

In this chapter, we will use Flask-Restless to create a RESTful API for the blogging app. A RESTful API is a way of accessing your blog programmatically, by providing highly structured data that represents your blog. Flask-Restless works very well with our SQLAlchemy models and also handles complex tasks such as serialization and result filtering. We will use our REST API to build an AJAX-powered commenting feature for our blog entries. By the end of this chapter, you will be able to create easily-configurable APIs for your SQLAlchemy models, and you'll make and respond to AJAX requests in your Flask app.

In this chapter we shall:

- Create a model to store comments on blog entries
- Install Flask-Restless
- Create a RESTful API for the comment model
- Build a frontend for communicating with our API using Ajax

## Creating a comment model

Before we start creating our API, we need to create a database model for the resource that we wish to share. The API we are building will be used to create and retrieve comments using AJAX, so our model will contain all the fields that would be relevant for storing an unauthenticated user's comment on one of our entries.

For our purposes, the following fields should be sufficient:

- name, the name of the person making the comment
- email, the e-mail address of the person commenting, which we will use solely to display an image of them from **Gravatar**
- URL, the URL to the commenters blog

- `ip_address`, the IP address of the commenter
- `body`, the actual comment
- `status`, one of either `Public`, `Spam`, or `Deleted`
- `created_timestamp`, the timestamp with which the comment was created
- `entry_id`, the ID of blog entry the comment relates to

Lets begin coding by creating the Comment model definition in our app's `models.py` module:

```python
class Comment(db.Model):
    STATUS_PENDING_MODERATION = 0
    STATUS_PUBLIC = 1
    STATUS_SPAM = 8
    STATUS_DELETED = 9

    id = db.Column(db.Integer, primary_key=True)
    name = db.Column(db.String(64))
    email = db.Column(db.String(64))
    url = db.Column(db.String(100))
    ip_address = db.Column(db.String(64))
    body = db.Column(db.Text)
    status = db.Column(db.SmallInteger, default=STATUS_PUBLIC)
    created_timestamp = db.Column(db.DateTime, default=datetime.
datetime.now)
    entry_id = db.Column(db.Integer, db.ForeignKey('entry.id'))

    def __repr__(self):
        return '<Comment from %r>' % (self.name,)
```

After adding the `Comment` model definition, we need to set up the SQLAlchemy relationship between the `Comment` and `Entry` models. As you will recall, we did this once before when setting up the relationship between `User` and `Entry` via the entries relationship. We will do this for `Comment` by adding a comments attribute to the `Entry` model.

Below the `tags` relationship, add the following code to the `Entry` model definition:

```python
class Entry(db.Model):
    # ...
    tags = db.relationship('Tag', secondary=entry_tags,
        backref=db.backref('entries', lazy='dynamic'))
    comments = db.relationship('Comment', backref='entry',
lazy='dynamic')
```

We've specified the relationship as `lazy='dynamic'`, which, as you will recall from *Chapter 5, Authenticating Users*, means that the `comments` attribute on any given `Entry` instance will be a filterable query.

# Creating a schema migration

In order to start using our new model, we need to update our database schema. Using the `manage.py` helper, create a schema migration for the `Comment` model:

```
(blog) $ python manage.py db migrate

INFO   [alembic.migration] Context impl SQLiteImpl.

INFO   [alembic.migration] Will assume non-transactional DDL.

INFO   [alembic.autogenerate.compare] Detected added table 'comment'

  Generating /home/charles/projects/blog/app/migrations/
versions/490b6bc5f73c_.py
... done
```

Then apply the migration by running `upgrade`:

```
(blog) $ python manage.py db upgrade

INFO   [alembic.migration] Context impl SQLiteImpl.

INFO   [alembic.migration] Will assume non-transactional DDL.

INFO   [alembic.migration] Running upgrade 594ebac9ef0c ->
490b6bc5f73c, empty message
```

The `Comment` model is now ready to use! At this point, if we were implementing comments using regular Flask views, we might create a comments blueprint and start writing a view to handle the comment creation. However, we will be exposing the comments using a REST API and create them using AJAX directly from the front-end.

# Installing Flask-Restless

With our model in place, we are now ready to install Flask-Restless, a third-party Flask extension that makes it simple to build RESTful APIs for your SQLAlchemy models. After ensuring that you have activated the blog app's virtual environment, install Flask-Restless using `pip`:

```
(blog) $ pip install Flask-Restless
```

You can verify if the extension is installed by opening up the interactive interpreter and getting the version that is installed. Don't forget, your exact version number may differ.

```
(blog) $ ./manage.py shell

In [1]: import flask_restless

In [2]: flask_restless.__version__
Out[2]: '0.13.0'
```

Now that we have Flask-Restless installed, let's configure it to work with our application.

# Setting up Flask-Restless

Like other Flask extensions, we will begin in the app.py module by configuring an object that will manage our new API. In Flask-Restless, this object is called an APIManager and it will allow us to create RESTful endpoints for our SQLAlchemy models. Add the following lines to app.py:

```
# Place this import at the top of the module alongside the other
extensions.
from flask.ext.restless import APIManager

# Place this line below the initialization of the app and db
objects.
api = APIManager(app, flask_sqlalchemy_db=db)
```

Because the API will depend on both our Flask API object and our Comment model, we need to make sure that we don't create any circular module dependencies. We can avoid introducing circular imports by creating a new module, api.py, at the root of the app directory.

Let's start with the bare minimum to see what Flask-Restless provides out-of-the-box. Add the following code to api.py:

```
from app import api
from models import Comment

api.create_api(Comment, methods=['GET', 'POST'])
```

The code in `api.py` calls the `create_api()` method on our `APIManager` object. This method will populate our app with additional URL routes and view code that, together, constitute a RESTful API. The methods parameter indicates that we will allow only `GET` and `POST` requests (meaning comments can be read or created, but not edited or deleted).

The final action is to import the new API module in `main.py`, the entry-point into our application. We are importing the module purely for its side-effects, registering the URL routes. Add the following code to `main.py`:

```
from app import app, db
import admin
import api
import models
import views

    . . .
```

# Making API requests

In one terminal, start up the development server. In another terminal, let's see what happens when we make a `GET` request to our API endpoint (note there is no trailing forward slash):

```
$ curl 127.0.0.1:5000/api/comment
{
  "num_results": 0,
  "objects": [],
  "page": 1,
  "total_pages": 0
}
```

There are no comments in the database, so no objects have been serialized and returned to us. However, there is some interesting metadata that tells us how many objects are there in the database, what page we are on, and how many total pages of comments exist.

Let's create a new comment by POSTing some JSON data to our API (I will assume that the first entry in your database has an id of 1). We will use `curl` to submit a POST request containing a JSON-encoded representation of a new comment:

```
$ curl -X POST -H "Content-Type: application/json" -d '{
    "name": "Charlie",
    "email": "charlie@email.com",
    "url": "http://charlesleifer.com",
    "ip_address": "127.0.0.1",
    "body": "Test comment!",
    "entry_id": 1}' http://127.0.0.1:5000/api/comment
```

Assuming that no typos were made, the API will respond with the following data, confirming the creation of the new `Comment`:

```
{
    "body": "Test comment!",
    "created_timestamp": "2014-04-22T19:48:33.724118",
    "email": "charlie@email.com",
    "entry": {
      "author_id": 1,
      "body": "This is an entry about Python, my favorite programming
language.",
      "created_timestamp": "2014-03-06T19:50:09",
      "id": 1,
      "modified_timestamp": "2014-03-06T19:50:09",
      "slug": "python-entry",
      "status": 0,
      "title": "Python Entry"
    },
    "entry_id": 1,
    "id": 1,
    "ip_address": "127.0.0.1",
    "name": "Charlie",
    "status": 0,
    "url": "http://charlesleifer.com"
}
```

As you can see, all the data we POSTed is included in the response, in addition to the rest of the field data, such as the new comment's id and timestamps. Surprisingly, even the corresponding `Entry` object has been serialized and included in the response.

Now that we have a comment in the database, let's try making another GET request to our API as follows:

```
$ curl 127.0.0.1:5000/api/comment
{
  "num_results": 1,
  "objects": [
    {
      "body": "Test comment!",
      "created_timestamp": "2014-04-22T19:48:33.724118",
      "email": "charlie@email.com",
      "entry": {
        "author_id": 1,
        "body": "This is an entry about Python, my favorite programming
language.",
        "created_timestamp": "2014-03-06T19:50:09",
        "id": 1,
        "modified_timestamp": "2014-03-06T19:50:09",
        "slug": "python-entry",
        "status": 0,
        "title": "Python Entry"
      },
      "entry_id": 1,
      "id": 1,
      "ip_address": "127.0.0.1",
      "name": "Charlie",
      "status": 0,
      "url": "http://charlesleifer.com"
    }
  ],
  "page": 1,
  "total_pages": 1
}
```

The first object contains exactly the same data that was returned to us when we made the POST request. In addition, the surrounding metadata has changed to reflect the fact that there is now one comment in the database.

# Creating comments using AJAX

In order to allow users to post comments, we first need a way to capture their input, which we will do by creating a Form class with wtforms. This form should allow users to enter their name, email address, an optional URL, and their comment.

In the forms module in the entries blueprint, add the following form definition:

```python
class CommentForm(wtforms.Form):
    name = wtforms.StringField('Name', validators=[validators.
DataRequired()])
    email = wtforms.StringField('Email', validators=[
        validators.DataRequired(),
        validators.Email()])
    url = wtforms.StringField('URL', validators=[
        validators.Optional(),
        validators.URL()])
    body = wtforms.TextAreaField('Comment', validators=[
        validators.DataRequired(),
        validators.Length(min=10, max=3000)])
    entry_id = wtforms.HiddenField(validators=[
        validators.DataRequired()])

    def validate(self):
        if not super(CommentForm, self).validate():
            return False

        # Ensure that entry_id maps to a public Entry.
        entry = Entry.query.filter(
            (Entry.status == Entry.STATUS_PUBLIC) &
            (Entry.id == self.entry_id.data)).first()
        if not entry:
            return False

        return True
```

You may be wondering why we are specifying validators, since the API will be handling the POSTed data. We do this because Flask-Restless does not provide validation, but it does provide a hook where we can perform validation. In this way, we can leverage WTForms validation inside our REST API.

In order to use the form in the entry detail page, we need to pass the form into the context when rendering the detail template. Open the entries blueprint and import the new CommentForm:

```
from entries.forms import EntryForm, ImageForm, CommentForm
```

Then modify the detail view to pass a form instance into the context. We will pre-populate the entry_id hidden field with the value of the requested entry:

```
@entries.route('/<slug>/')
def detail(slug):
    entry = get_entry_or_404(slug)
    form = CommentForm(data={'entry_id': entry.id})
    return render_template('entries/detail.html', entry=entry,
form=form)
```

With the form now in the detail template context, all that is left is to render the form. Create an empty template in entries/templates/entries/includes/ named comment_form.html and add the following code:

```
{% from "macros/form_field.html" import form_field %}
<form action="/api/comment" class="form form-horizontal" id="comment-
form" method="post">
  {{ form_field(form.name) }}
  {{ form_field(form.email) }}
  {{ form_field(form.url) }}
  {{ form_field(form.body) }}
  {{ form.entry_id() }}
  <div class="form-group">
    <div class="col-sm-offset-3 col-sm-9">
      <button type="submit" class="btn btn-default">Submit</button>
    </div>
  </div>
</form>
```

The interesting thing to note is that we are not using the form_field macro for the entry_id field. This is because we do not want the comment form to display a label for a field that will not be visible to the user. Instead, we will initialize the form with this value.

Lastly, we need to include the comment form in the `detail.html` template. Below the entry body, add the following markup:

```
{% block content %}
  {{ entry.body }}

  <h4 id="comment-form">Submit a comment</h4>
  {% include "entries/includes/comment_form.html" %}
{% endblock %}
```

Using the development server, try navigating to the detail page for any entry. You should see a comment form:

# AJAX form submissions

To simplify making AJAX requests, we are going to use the jQuery library. Feel free to substitute another JavaScript library if you prefer but, since jQuery is so ubiquitous (and plays nicely with Bootstrap), we will be using it for this section. If you have been following along with the code up to this point, jQuery should already be included on all pages. Now we need to create a JavaScript file to handle the comment submission.

Create a new file in `statics/js/` named `comments.js` and add the following JavaScript code:

```
Comments = window.Comments || {};

(function(exports, $) {
  /* Template string for rendering success or error messages. */
  var alertMarkup = (
    '<div class="alert alert-{class} alert-dismissable">' +
    '<button type="button" class="close" data-dismiss="alert"
aria-hidden="true">&times;</button>' +
    '<strong>{title}</strong> {body}</div>');

  /* Create an alert element. */
  function makeAlert(alertClass, title, body) {
    var alertCopy = (alertMarkup
                    .replace('{class}', alertClass)
                    .replace('{title}', title)
                    .replace('{body}', body));
    return $(alertCopy);
  }


  /* Retrieve the values from the form fields and return as an
object. */
  function getFormData(form) {
    return {
      'name': form.find('input#name').val(),
      'email': form.find('input#email').val(),
      'url': form.find('input#url').val(),
      'body': form.find('textarea#body').val(),
      'entry_id': form.find('input[name=entry_id]').val()
    }
  }


  function bindHandler() {
    /* When the comment form is submitted, serialize the form data
as JSON
             and POST it to the API. */
    $('form#comment-form').on('submit', function() {
      var form = $(this);
      var formData = getFormData(form);
      var request = $.ajax({
        url: form.attr('action'),
```

```
        type: 'POST',
        data: JSON.stringify(formData),
        contentType: 'application/json; charset=utf-8',
        dataType: 'json'
      });
      request.success(function(data) {
        alertDiv = makeAlert('success', 'Success', 'your comment
was posted.');
        form.before(alertDiv);
        form[0].reset();
      });
      request.fail(function() {
        alertDiv = makeAlert('danger', 'Error', 'your comment was
not posted.');
        form.before(alertDiv);
      });
      return false;
    });
  }

  exports.bindHandler = bindHandler;
})(Comments, jQuery);
```

The `comments.js` code handles POSTing the form data, serialized as JSON, to the REST API. It also handles taking the API response and displaying either a success or an error message.

In the `detail.html` template, we simply need to include our script and bind the submit handler. Add the following block override to the detail template:

```
{% block extra_scripts %}
  <script type="text/javascript" src="{{ url_for('static',
filename='js/comments.js') }}"></script>
  <script type="text/javascript">
    $(function() {
      Comments.bindHandler();
    });
  </script>
{% endblock %}
```

Go ahead and try submitting a comment or two.

# Validating data in the API

Unfortunately for us, our API is not performing any type of validation on the incoming data. In order to validate the POST data, we need to use a hook provided by Flask-Restless. Flask-Restless calls these hooks request preprocessors and postprocessors.

Let's take a look at how to use the POST preprocessor to perform some validation on our comment data. Start by opening api.py and making the following changes:

```python
from flask.ext.restless import ProcessingException

from app import api
from entries.forms import CommentForm
from models import Comment


def post_preprocessor(data, **kwargs):
    form = CommentForm(data=data)
    if form.validate():
        return form.data
    else:
        raise ProcessingException(
            description='Invalid form submission.',
            code=400)

api.create_api(
    Comment,
    methods=['GET', 'POST'],
    preprocessors={
        'POST': [post_preprocessor],
    })
```

Our API will now validate the submitted comment using the validation logic from our CommentForm. We do this by specifying a preprocessor for the POST method. The POST preprocessor, which we've implemented as post_preprocessor, accepts the deserialized POST data as an argument. We can then feed that data into our CommentForm and call it's validate() method. In the event where validation fails, we will raise a ProcessingException, signaling to Flask-Restless that this data was unprocessable and returning a 400 Bad Request response.

In the following screenshot, I have not supplied the **Comment** field, which is required. I receive an error message when I try to submit the comment:

---

**Submit a comment**

> **Error** your comment was not posted.                                    ✕

| | |
|---:|:---|
| **Name** | Charlie |
| **Email** | charlie@email.com |
| **URL** | |
| **Comment** | |
| | Submit |

---

# Preprocessors and postprocessors

We just looked at an example of using the POST method preprocessor with Flask-Restless. In the following table, you can see the other hooks that are available:

| Method name | Description | Preprocessor arguments | Postprocessor arguments |
|---|---|---|---|
| GET_SINGLE | Retrieve a single object by primary key | instance_id, the primary key of the object | result, the dictionary representation of the object |
| GET_MANY | Retrieve multiple objects | search_params, a dictionary of search parameters used to filter the result set | result, the representation of the object's search_params |
| PUT_SINGLE | Update a single object by primary key | instance_id<br><br>data, a dictionary of data used to update the object | result, the dictionary representation of the updated object |

| Method name | Description | Preprocessor arguments | Postprocessor arguments |
|---|---|---|---|
| PUT_MANY | Update multiple objects | search_params, a dictionary of search parameters used to determine which objects to update.<br><br>data, a dictionary of data used to update the object. | query, a SQLAlchemy query representing the objects to be updated.<br><br>data<br><br>search_params |
| POST | Create a new instance | data, the dictionary of data to populate the new object | result, a dictionary representation of the new object |
| DELETE | Delete an instance by primary key | instance_id, the primary key of the object to be deleted | was_deleted, a boolean value indicating whether the object was deleted |

# Loading comments using AJAX

Now that we are able to create validated comments using AJAX, let's use the API to retrieve the list of comments and display them beneath the blog entry. To do this, we will read the values from the API and dynamically create DOM elements to display the comments. As you might recall from the earlier API responses we examined, there is quite a bit of private information being returned, including the entire serialized representation of each comment's associated Entry. For our purposes, this information is redundant and will furthermore waste bandwidth.

Let's begin by doing a bit of additional configuration to our comments endpoint to restrict the Comment fields we return. In api.py, make the following addition to the call to api.create_api():

```
api.create_api(
    Comment,
    include_columns=['id', 'name', 'url', 'body',
'created_timestamp'],
    methods=['GET', 'POST'],
    preprocessors={
        'POST': [post_preprocessor],
    })
```

Requesting the list of comments now gives us a more manageable response that doesn't leak implementation details or private data:

```
$ curl http://127.0.0.1:5000/api/comment
{
  "num_results": 1,
  "objects": [
    {
      "body": "Test comment!",
      "created_timestamp": "2014-04-22T19:48:33.724118",
      "name": "Charlie",
      "url": "http://charlesleifer.com"
    }
  ],
  "page": 1,
  "total_pages": 1
}
```

A nice feature would be to display an avatar next to a user's comment. Gravatar, a free avatar service, allows users to associate their e-mail address with an image. We will use the commenter's e-mail address to display their associated avatar (if one exists). If the user has not created an avatar, an abstract pattern will be shown instead.

Let's add a method on the `Comment` model to generate the URL for a user's Gravatar image. Open `models.py` and add the following method to `Comment`:

```
def gravatar(self, size=75):
    return 'http://www.gravatar.com/avatar.php?%s' % urllib.urlencode({
        'gravatar_id': hashlib.md5(self.email).hexdigest(),
        'size': str(size)})
```

You will also need to be sure to import `hashlib` and `urllib` at the top of the models module.

If we attempt to include Gravatar in the list of columns, Flask-Restless will raise an exception because `gravatar` is actually a method. Luckily, Flask-Restless provides a way to include the results of method calls when serializing objects. In `api.py`, make the following addition to the `create_api()` call:

```
api.create_api(
    Comment,
    include_columns=['id', 'name', 'url', 'body', 'created_
timestamp'],
    include_methods=['gravatar'],
    methods=['GET', 'POST'],#, 'DELETE'],
    preprocessors={
        'POST': [post_preprocessor],
    })
```

Go ahead and try fetching the list of comments. You should now see the Gravatar URL included in the serialized response.

# Retrieving the list of comments

We now need to return to our JavaScript file and add code to retrieve the list of comments. We will do this by passing in a search filter to the API, which will retrieve only the comments that are associated with the requested blog entry. Search queries are expressed as a list of filters, each filter specifying the following:

- Name of the column
- Operation (for example, equals)
- Value to search for

Open `comments.js` and add the following code after the line that begins:

```
(function(exports, $) {:
function displayNoComments() {
  noComments = $('<h3>', {
    'text': 'No comments have been posted yet.'});
  $('h4#comment-form').before(noComments);
}

/* Template string for rendering a comment. */
var commentTemplate = (
  '<div class="media">' +
    '<a class="pull-left" href="{url}">' +
```

```
          '<img class="media-object" src="{gravatar}" />' +
      '</a>' +
      '<div class="media-body">' +
      '<h4 class="media-heading">{created_timestamp}</h4>{body}' +
    '</div></div>'
);

function renderComment(comment) {
  var createdDate = new Date(comment.created_timestamp).
toDateString();
  return (commentTemplate
            .replace('{url}', comment.url)
            .replace('{gravatar}', comment.gravatar)
            .replace('{created_timestamp}', createdDate)
            .replace('{body}', comment.body));
}


function displayComments(comments) {
  $.each(comments, function(idx, comment) {
    var commentMarkup = renderComment(comment);
    $('h4#comment-form').before($(commentMarkup));
  });
}

function load(entryId) {
  var filters = [{
    'name': 'entry_id',
    'op': 'eq',
    'val': entryId}];
  var serializedQuery = JSON.stringify({'filters': filters});

  $.get('/api/comment', {'q': serializedQuery}, function(data) {
    if (data['num_results'] === 0) {
      displayNoComments();
    } else {
      displayComments(data['objects']);
    }
  });
}
```

Then, near the bottom of the file, export the load function alongside the `bindHandler` export as follows:

```
exports.load = load;
exports.bindHandler = bindHandler;
```

The new JavaScript code that we added makes an AJAX request to the API for comments associated with a given Entry. If no comments exist, a message is displayed indicating no comments have been made yet. Otherwise, the entries are rendered as a list below the `Entry` body.

The final task left is to call `Comments.load()` in the details template when the page is rendered. Open `detail.html` and add the following highlighted code:

```
<script type="text/javascript">
  $(function() {
    Comments.load({{ entry.id }});
    Comments.bindHandler();
  });
</script>
```

After making a couple comments, the comment list looks as seen in the following image:

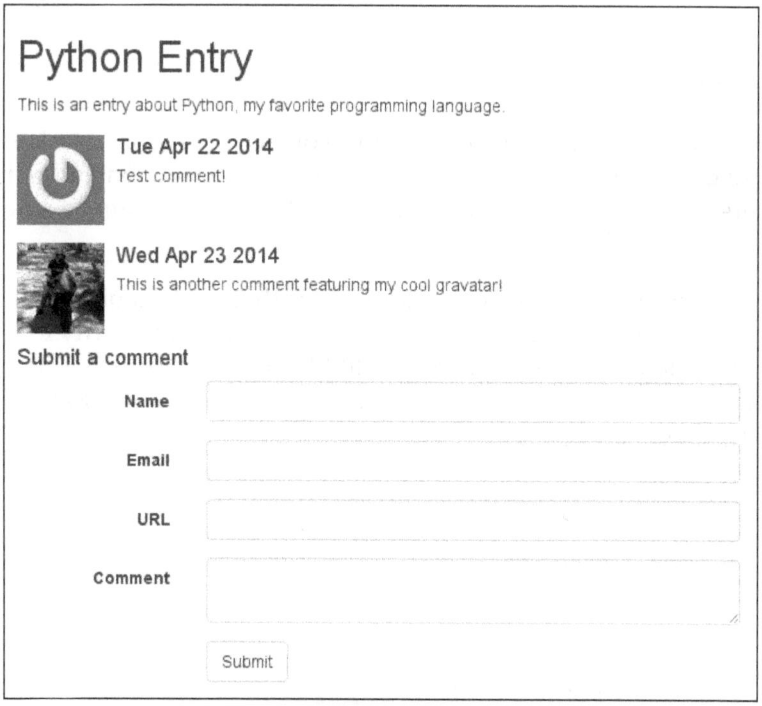

As an exercise, see if you can write code to render any new comment that is POSTed by the user. You will recall that, when a comment is successfully created, the new data will be returned as a JSON object.

# Reading more

Flask-Restless supports a number of configuration options that, in the interests of space, could not be covered in this chapter. The search filters are a very powerful tool, and we only scratched the surface of what is possible. Additionally, the pre and postprocessing hooks can be used to implement a number of interesting features such as the following:

- Authentication, which can be implemented in the preprocessor
- Default filters for GET_MANY, which could be used to restrict the list of comments to those that are public, for instance
- Adding custom or calculated values to the serialized response
- Modifying incoming POST values to set default values on the model instance

If REST API is a key component in your application, I strongly suggest spending time reading the Flask-Restless documentation. The documentation can be found online at https://flask-restless.readthedocs.org/en/latest/.

# Summary

In this chapter, we added a simple REST API to our app using the Flask-Restless extension. We then used JavaScript and Ajax to integrate our frontend with the API, allowing users to view and post new comments, all without writing a single line of view code.

In our next chapter, we will work on creating apps that are testable and find ways to improve our code for this purpose. This will also allow us to verify that the code we have written is doing what we would like it to do; nothing more, nothing less. Automating this will give you confidence and ensure that the RESTful API is working as expected.

# 8
# Testing Flask Apps

In this chapter, we shall learn how to write unit tests covering all parts of the blogging app. We will utilize Flask's test client to simulate live requests, and we will see how the Mock library can simplify the testing of complex interactions, such as calling third-party services such as databases.

In this chapter we shall learn the following topics:

- Python's unit test module and general guidelines for test writing
- Test-friendly configuration
- How to simulate requests and sessions using the Flask test client
- How to use the Mock library to test complex interactions
- Logging exceptions and error e-mails

## Unit testing

Unit Testing is a process that allows us to have confidence in the code, confidence in bug fixes, and confidence in future features. The idea of unit testing is simple; you write code that complements your functional code.

As an example, let's say we design a program that needs to calculate some math correctly; how do you know it's successful? Why not pull out a calculator, and you know what a computer is? A big calculator. Also, computers are really quite good at mundane repetitive tasks, so why not write a unit test that works out the answer for you? Repeat this pattern for all areas of your code, bundle those tests up into one wrapper, and you have complete confidence in the code that you have produced.

> There are some who say that tests are a sign of code "smell", that your code is so complex that it needs tests to prove that it works. This means that the code should be simpler. However, it really depends on your situation and it is up to you to make that judgment call. Unit tests are a good place to start before we start getting into making the code simpler.

What is clever about unit testing is that the tests complement the functional code. The methods prove that the tests work and the tests prove that the methods work. It reduces the likelihood of the code having major functional bugs, reducing the headache of having to rework the code in future, and allows you to concentrate on the minutiae of the new features that you want to work on.

> The idea behind unit tests is to verify that small sections of code – or rather, simple bits of functionality – are tested. This will then build to the greater whole of your application. It is very easy to end up writing enormous tests that test the functionality of your code and not the code itself. If your test is looking pretty big, it's usually an indication that your main code should be broken down into smaller methods.

# Python's unit test module

Fortunately, as is almost always the case with Python, there is a built-in unit test module. Much like Flask, it's very easy to get a simple unit test module in place. In your main blog app, create a new directory called `tests` and, within that directory, create a new file called `test.py`. Now, using your favorite text editor, enter in the following code:

```python
import unittest

class ExampleTest(unittest.TestCase):
  def setUp(self):
    pass

  def tearDown(self):
    pass

  def test_some_functionality(self):
    pass

  def test_some_other_functionality(self):
```

```
    pass

if __name__ == "__main__":
    unittest.main()
```

The preceding snippet demonstrates the basic framework for all the unit test modules that we will write. Simply making use of the built-in Python module `unittest`, it then creates a class that wraps a particular set of tests. The tests in this example, are the methods that start with the word `test`. The unit test module recognizes these as the methods that should be run each time `unittest.main` is called. Also, the `TestCase` class, which the `ExampleTest` class is inheriting from here, has some special methods that unit test will always attempt to use. One of them is `setUp`, a method that is run before each of the test methods that are run. This can be particularly useful when you want to run each test in isolation, but want, for example, to have a connection to a database in place.

The other special method is `tearDown`. This is run whenever a test method is run. Again, this is extremely useful for running each test in isolation when we want to maintain a database.

Obviously, this code example will not do anything if run. To get it to a usable state, and by following the principles of **test-driven development** (TDD), we first need to write a test that verifies that the code we are going to write works correctly and then write the code that fulfills that test.

# A simple math test

For this example, we are going to write a test that verifies that a method will accept two numbers as arguments, subtract one from the second argument, then multiply them together. Take a look at the following example:

| Argument 1 | Argument 2 | Answer |
|------------|------------|--------|
| 1 | 1 | 1 * (1-1) = 0 |
| 1 | 2 | 1 * (2-1) = 1 |
| 2 | 3 | 2 * (3-1) = 4 |

In your `test.py` file, you can create a method within the `ExampleTest` class that represents the preceding table as follows:

```
def test_minus_one_multiplication(self):
    self.assertEqual(my_multiplication(1,1), 0)
    self.assertEqual(my_multiplication(1,2), 1)
    self.assertEqual(my_multiplication(2,3), 4)
    self.assertNotEqual(my_multiplication(2,2), 3)
```

The preceding code creates a new method that asserts, with Python's `unittest` module, the answers to the questions. The `assertEqual` function takes the returned response from the `my_multiplication` method on the first argument and compares that to the second argument. If it passes, it does nothing, waiting for the next assertion to be tested. But if it does not match, it will throw an error and your test method will stop executing to tell you there was an error.

In the preceding code example, there is also an `assertNotEqual` method. This works much the same as `assertEqual` but, rather, checks whether the values do not match each other. It is also a good idea to check when your method is likely to fail. If you've only checked the situations in which your method will work, you have only done half the work, and will likely run into problems with edge cases. A wide variety of assertion methods come with Python's `unittest` module, and that would be useful to explore.

Now we can write the method that will give these results. For simplicity, we will write the method in the same file. Within the file, create the following method:

```
def my_multiplication(value1, value2):
    return value1 * value2 - 1
```

Save the file and run it using the following command:

**python test.py**

```
[matt@u36sd-localdomain 08]$ python test.py
F..
=====================================================================
FAIL: test_minus_one_multiplication (__main__.ExampleTest)
---------------------------------------------------------------------
Traceback (most recent call last):
  File "test.py", line 19, in test_minus_one_multiplication
    self.assertEqual(my_multiplication(2,3), 4)
AssertionError: 5 != 4


---------------------------------------------------------------------
Ran 3 tests in 0.001s

FAILED (failures=1)
[matt@u36sd-localdomain 08]$ █
```

Oops! It failed. Why? Well, reviewing the `my_multiplication` method reveals that we missed some brackets. Let's go back and correct that:

```
def my_multiplication(value1, value2):
    return value1 * (value2 - 1)
```

And now lets run it again:

```
[matt@u36sd-localdomain 08]$ python test.py
...
---------------------------------------------------------------------
Ran 3 tests in 0.000s

OK
```

Success! We now have a method that is correct; in future, we will know if it has been changed, and how it will need to be changed at a later point. Now to use this new skill with Flask.

# Flask and unit testing

You may be thinking: "Unit tests look great for small sections of code, but how do you test it for an entire Flask app?" Well one of the ways, as mentioned previously, is to make sure that all your methods are as discrete as possible—that is, to make sure your methods do the least possible work to complete their function, and to avoid repetition between methods. If your methods are not discrete, now is a good time to get them tidied up.

Another thing that will help is that Flask comes readymade for unit testing. There is a good chance that any existing application can have at least some unit tests applied to it. Especially, any areas of API such as in unable to verify will be extremely easy to test by making use of the methods that represent the HTTP requests already within Flask. Following is a simple example:

```python
import unittest
from flask import request
from main import app

class AppTest(unittest.TestCase):
    def setUp(self):
        self.app = app.test_client()

    def test_homepage_works(self):
        response = self.app.get("/")
        self.assertEqual(response.status_code, 200)

if __name__ == "__main__":
    unittest.main()
```

This code should hopefully look very familiar. It simply re-writes the previous example to verify that the homepage is working. The test_client method that Flask exposes, allows simple access to the app via methods that represent the HTTP calls, as per the first line of the test method. The test method itself does not check the content of the page, but simply that the page loaded successfully. This may sound trivial, but it is useful to know that the homepage works. And the result? You can see it here:

```
[matt@u36sd-localdomain app]$ python test.py
.
- - - - - - - - - - - - - - - - - - - - - - - - - - - - - - - - - - - - - - - -
Ran 1 test in 0.025s

OK
[matt@u36sd-localdomain app]$
```

> One thing to be aware of is that we won't need to test Flask itself and must avoid testing it so that we don't create too much work for ourselves.

# Testing a page

One thing to notice about running the previous tests are that they are very simplistic. No actual browser behaves that way. Browsers do things such as storing cookies for logging in: requesting static files such as JavaScript, images, and CSS files: and requesting data in particular formats. Somehow, we are going to need to simulate this functionality and test whether the results were correct.

> This is the part where unit testing starts becoming functional testing. While there is nothing intrinsically wrong with that, it is worth keeping in mind that smaller tests are better.

Fortunately, Flask does all this for you simply by using the `app.get` methods from earlier, but there are some tricks you can use to make things easier. For example, adding functions to the `TestCase` class for logging in and out will make things much simpler:

```
LOGIN_URL = "/login/"
LOGOUT_URL = "/logout/"

def login (self, email, password):
    return self.app.post(self.LOGIN_URL, data={
        "email": email,
        "password": password
    }, follow_redirects=True)
```

The preceding code is a framework for future test cases. Any time we have a test case that requires logging in and out, add this `Mixin` to the inheritance list and it automatically becomes available:

```
class ExampleFlaskTest(unittest.TestCase, FlaskLoginMixin):
  def setUp(self):
    self.app = app.test_client()

  def test_login(self):
    response = self.login("admin", "password")
    self.assertEqual(response.status_code, 200)
    self.assertTrue("Success" in response.data)

  def test_failed_login(self):
    response = self.login("admin", "PASSWORD")
```

```
        self.assertEqual(response.status_code, 200)
        self.assertTrue("Invalid" in response.data)

    def test_logout(self):
      response = self.logout()
      self.assertEqual(response.status_code, 200)
      self.assertTrue("logged out" in response.data)
```

The test case that we've just explained uses `FlaskLoginMixin`, a set of methods that aid in checking whether logging in and out is working correctly. This is achieved by checking that the response page sends the correct message and has the correct warning in the content of the page. Our test can further be extended to check whether a user has access to a page which they shouldn't. Flask takes care of the sessions and cookies for you, so it's as simple as the following code snippet:

```
class ExampleFlaskTest(unittest.TestCase, FlaskLoginMixin):
  def setUp(self):
    self.app = app.test_client()

  def test_admin_can_get_to_admin_page(self):
    self.login("admin", "password")
    response = self.app.get("/admin/")
    self.assertEqual(response.status_code, 200)
    self.assertTrue("Hello" in response.data)

  def test_non_logged_in_user_can_get_to_admin_page(self):
    response = self.app.get("/admin/")
    self.assertEqual(response.status_code, 302)
    self.assertTrue("redirected" in response.data)

  def test_normal_user_cannot_get_to_admin_page(self):
    self.login("user", "password")
    response = self.app.get("/admin/")
    self.assertEqual(response.status_code, 302)
    self.assertTrue("redirected" in response.data)

  def test_logging_out_prevents_access_to_admin_page(self):
    self.login("admin", "password")
    self.logout()
    response = self.app.get("/admin/")
    self.assertEqual(response.status_code, 302)
    self.assertTrue("redirected" in response.data)
```

What the preceding code snippet shows is how to test whether certain pages are correctly protected. A very useful test. It also verifies that, when an admin logs out, they can no longer access the pages they had access to while being logged in. The method names are self, explanatory such that if those tests fail, it is obvious to tell what was being tested.

# Testing an API

Testing APIs is even easier as it is a programmatic interference. Using the previous comment API set up in *Chapter 7, AJAX and RESTful APIs,* we can quite easily insert and retrieve some comments and verify that it worked correctly. To test this we will need to import the json library to work with our JSON based API:

```
class ExampleFlaskAPITest(unittest.TestCase, FlaskLoginMixin):
  def setUp(self):
    self.app = app.test_client()
    self.comment_data = {
      "name": "admin",
      "email": "admin@example.com",
      "url": "http://localhost",
      "ip_address": "127.0.0.1",
      "body": "test comment!",
      "entry_id": 1
    }

  def test_adding_comment(self):
    self.login("admin", "password")
      data=json.dumps(self.comment_data), content_type="application/
json")
    self.assertEqual(response.status_code, 200)
    self.assertTrue("body" in response.data)
    self.assertEqual(json.loads(response.data)['body'], self.comment_
data["body"])

  def test_getting_comment(self):
            result = self.app.post("/api/comment",
            data=json.dumps(self.comment_data), content_
type="application/json")
        response = self.app.get("/api/comment")
        self.assertEqual(response.status_code, 200)
        self.assertTrue(json.loads(result.data) in json.
loads(response.data)['objects'])
```

The preceding code example shows a comment dictionary object being created. This is used to verify that the values that went in were the same as the ones that came out. The methods therefore test posting the comment data to the `/api/comment` endpoint, verifying the data that sent back by the server has the right data in it. The `test_getting_comment` method checks again that a comment is posted to the server but is more concerned if the result that was requested by verifying the data that was sent in was the same as what came out.

# Test-friendly configuration

One of the first obstacles faced by writing tests in a team or with a production environment is, How do we make sure that the tests are run without interfering with the production or even the development database. You certainly don't want to be attempting to fix bugs, or trialing new features and then finding that the data it relies upon has changed. Sometimes, a quick test just needs to be run on a local copy of the database without interference from anyone else, with the Flask app knowing how to use that.

One of the features built into Flask is the ability to load a configuration file depending on the environment variables.

```
app.config.from_envvar('FLASK_APP_BLOG_CONFIG_FILE')
```

The preceding method call informs your Flask app that the configuration should be loaded in the file specified in the environment variable `FLASK_APP_BLOG_CONFIG_FILE`. This has to be an absolute path to the file that you would like to load. Therefore, when you run your tests, a file specific to running your tests should be referred to here.

As we already have a configuration file set up for our environment and we are looking to create a testing configuration file, a useful trick is to make use of the existing configuration and override just the important bits. The first thing to do is to create yourself a config directory with an __init__.py file. Our testing.py configuration file can then be added to that directory and can override some aspects of your config.py configuration file. For example, your new testing configuration file might look as follows:

```
TESTING=True
DATABASE="sqlite://
```

The preceding code adds the TESTING attribute that can be used to determine if your app is currently being tested, and changes the DATABASE value to a database that is more suitable for testing, an in-memory SQLite database that doesn't have to be cleared down once your test finishes

These values can then be used like any other configuration in Flask and, when running the tests, the environment variable can be specified to point to that file. If we want to automate the updating of the environment variable for our tests, we can update Python's built-in OS environment variable object in our `test.py` file in the `test` folder:

```
import os
os.environ['FLASK_APP_BLOG_CONFIG_FILE'] = os.path.join(os.getcwd(),
"config", "testing.py")
```

# Mocking objects

Mocking is an exceptionally useful part of any tester's tool kit. Mocking allows for custom objects to be over written with an object that can be used to verify if a method is doing the correct thing to its arguments. Sometimes, this may need a bit of re-imagining and a refactoring of your app so as to work in a testable way, but otherwise the concept is simple. We create a mocking object, run it through the method, and then run the tests on that object. It lends itself particularly well to databases and ORM models such as from `SQLAlchemy`.

There are lots of Mocking frameworks available but, for this book, we shall be using `Mockito`:

```
pip install mockito
```

It is one of the simplest to use:

```
>>> from mockito import *
>>> mock_object = mock()
>>> mock_object.example()
>>> verify(mock_object).example()
True
```

The preceding code imports the functions from the `Mockito` library, creates a `mock` object that can be used for mocking, runs a method on it, and verifies that the method has been run. Obviously, if you want the method being tested to function properly without an error, you will need it to return a valid value when the method on the mocked object is being called.

```
>>> duck = mock()
>>> when(duck).quack().thenReturn("quack")
>>> duck.quack()
"quack"
```

In the preceding example, we are creating a mocked up `duck` object, giving it the ability to `quack`, and then proving that it can `quack`.

> In dynamically typed languages such as Python, where an object you have may not be the one you are expecting, it is common practice to use duck-typing. As the phrase says "if it walks like a duck and quacks like a duck, it must be a duck". This is really useful when creating mocking objects, as it is easy to use a fake Mock object without your methods noticing the switch.

The difficulty arises when Flask uses its decorators to run methods before your method is run and you need to override it to, for example, replace the database initiator. The technique that can be used here is to have the decorators run a method that is globally available to the module, such as a method that creates a connection to the database.

Say your `app.py` looks like the following:

```
from flask import Flask, g

app = Flask("example")

def get_db():
  return {}

@app.before_request
def setup_db():
  g.db = get_db()

@app.route("/")
def homepage():
    return g.db.get("foo")
```

The preceding code sets up a very simple app that creates a fake database as a Python dictionary object. Now to override with our own database as follows:

```
from mockito import *
import unittest
import app

class FlaskExampleTest(unittest.TestCase):
  def setUp(self):
    self.app = app.app.test_client()
    self.db = mock()
    def get_fake_db():
      return self.db
    app.get_db =  get_fake_db

  def test_before_request_override(self):
    when(self.db).get("foo").thenReturn("123")
    response = self.app.get("/")
    self.assertEqual(response.status_code, 200)
    self.assertEqual(response.data,  "123")

if __name__ == "__main__":
  unittest.main()
```

The preceding code uses the Mockito library to create a fake database object. It also creates a method that overrides the method in the app module that creates the connection to the database — in this case, a simple dictionary object. You will notice that you can also specify arguments for methods when using Mockito. Now when the test is run, it inserts a value into the database for the page to return; this is then tested.

# Logging and error reporting

Logging and error reporting are intrinsic to a production-ready web app. Logging keeps a record of all problems even if your app has crashed, while error reporting can directly notify us of specific problems even though the site keeps running.

It can be very gratifying to discover errors before anyone has reported them. It also makes it possible to roll out fixes before your users start complaining to you. However, to do this, you need to know what those errors were, when they occurred, and what caused them.

Fortunately, as must be quite familiar right now, Python and Flask already have this in hand.

# Logging

Flask comes with a built-in logger — an already defined instance of Python's built-in logger. You will hopefully be quite familiar with it by now. The logger messages are displayed, by default, each time a page is accessed.

```
[matt@u36sd-localdomain app]$ python app.py
 * Running on http://127.0.0.1:5000/
127.0.0.1 - - [22/Dec/2014 17:30:18] "GET / HTTP/1.1" 200 -
127.0.0.1 - - [22/Dec/2014 17:30:23] "GET /admin HTTP/1.1" 404 -
127.0.0.1 - - [22/Dec/2014 17:30:30] "GET /static HTTP/1.1" 404 -
```

The preceding screenshot, obviously, shows the output to the terminal. We can see here that someone accessed the root page from localhost (127.0.0.1), on that particular date, with a GET request, as well as a few other directories. The server responded with one '200 success' message, and two '404 not found error' messages. While having this terminal output is useful when developing, it is not necessarily very useful if your app crashed while running in your production environment. We will need to see what happened from a file that was written to.

# Logging to file

There are various OS, dependent ways of writing logs like this to a file. However, as indicated previously, Python does have this built in, and Flask simply follows Python's plan, which is quite simple. Add the following to the app.py file:

```
from logging.handlers import RotatingFileHandler
file_handler = RotatingFileHandler('blog.log')
app.logger.addHandler(file_handler)
```

One thing to note here is that loggers make use of different handlers to complete their functionality. The handler we are using here is RotatingFileHandler. Not only does this handler write the files to disk (in this case to blog.log) Courier but also makes sure that our file doesn't get too big and fills up the disk with log messages, potentially taking the site down.

# Custom log messages

One thing that can be really useful when trying to debug a difficult-to-trace issue is that we can add more logging to our blogging app. This can be done with the built-in logging object within Flask as follows:

```
@app.route("/")
def homepage():
    app.logger.info("Homepage has been accessed.")
```

The preceding example demonstrates how to create a custom logging message. However, a message such as this will actually slow down our application quite considerably as it will write that message to the file or to the console, each time the homepage is accessed. Fortunately, Flask also understands the concept of logging levels, whereby we can specify which messages should be logged in different environments. For example, it would not be useful to record a message such as an info message in a production environment whereas a user failing to log in would be worthy of recording.

```
app.logger.warning("'{user}' failed to login successfully.".format(us
er=user))
```

The preceding command simply logs a warning that a user failed to log in successfully using Python's string format method. As long as the error logging is low enough in Python, this message will be displayed.

# Levels

The principle of logging levels is: the higher the importance of the log, the higher the level, and the less likely it is to be logged, depending on your logging level. For example, to be able to log warnings (and above, such as ERROR), we need to adjust the logging level to WARNING. We can do this in our configuration file. Edit the config.py file in the config folder to add the following:

```
import logging
LOG_LEVEL=logging.WARNING
Now in your app.py add the line:
app.logger.setLevel(config['LOG_LEVEL'])
```

The preceding code snippet just uses the built-in Python logger to tell Flask how to handle logs. Of course, you can set different logging levels depending on your environment. For example, in your testing.py file in the config folder, we should use the following:

```
LOG_LEVEL=logging.ERROR
```

As for the purpose of testing, we don't need warnings. Similarly, we should do this for any production configuration file; for any development configuration files, use style.

# Error reporting

It's all well and good having errors logged on the machine but it's even better if the errors come straight to your inbox where you can be immediately notified. Fortunately, as with all these things, Python has a built-in way of doing it that Flask can make use of. It is just another handler such as `RotatingFileHandler`.

```
from logging.handlers import SMTPHandler
email_handler = SMTPHandler("127.0.0.1", "admin@localhost",
app.config['ADMIN_EMAILS'], "{appname}
error".format(appname=app.name))
app.logger.addHandler(email_handler)
```

The preceding code creates `SMTPHandler` with a configuration that identifies where your mail server is and what the send address is, takes a list of e-mail addresses to send to from the configuration file, and gives the e-mail a subject so that we can identify where the error came from.

# Read more

Unit testing is a vast and complex area. Flask has some excellent documentation on other techniques for writing effective tests: `http://flask.pocoo.org/docs/0.10/testing/`.

Python, of course, has its own documentation on unit testing: `https://docs.python.org/2/library/unittest.html`.

Flask uses the logging module from Python for its logging. This, in turn, follows the C library structure for its logging levels. More detail can be found at: `https://docs.python.org/2/library/logging.html`.

# Summary

In this chapter, we have learnt how to create some tests for our blogging app to verify that it is loading pages correctly, and that logging-in is taking place correctly. We have also set up logging to files and sent e-mails when errors occur.

In the next chapter, we will learn how we can improve our blog with extensions that add extra features with minimal effort on our part.

# 9
# Excellent Extensions

In this chapter, we will learn about enhancing our Flask install with some popular third-party extensions. Extensions allow us to add extra security or functionality with very little effort and can polish your blogging app nicely. We will investigate **Cross-Site Request Forgery (CSRF)** protection for your forms, Atom feeds so others can find your blog updates, adding syntax highlighting to the code that you use, caching to reduce the load when rendering templates, and asynchronous tasks so that your app doesn't become unresponsive when it is doing something intensive.

In this chapter we shall learn the following:

- CSRF protection using Flask-SeaSurf
- Atom feeds using werkzeug.contrib
- Syntax highlighting using Pygments
- Caching using Flask-Cache and Redis
- Asynchronous task execution using Celery

## SeaSurf and CSRF protection of forms

CSRF protection adds security to your site by proving that a POST submission came from your site, and not a carefully crafted web form on another site designed to maliciously exploit the POST endpoints on your blog. These malicious requests can even work around authentication if your browser still considers you logged in.

The way we avoid this is to add a special hidden field to any form on the site that has a value in it, generated by the server. When the form is submitted, the value in the special field can then be checked against the values generated by the server and, if it matches, we can continue with the form submission. If the value does not match or is non-existent, the form has come from an invalid source.

> What CSRF protection actually proves is that the template, with the CSRF field in it, was used to generate the form. This mitigates the most basic of CSRF attacks from other sites but isn't conclusive in validating that the form submission only came from our server. For example, a script could still screen-scrape the contents of the page.

Now, it would be simple to build CSRF protection ourselves and WTForms, which is typically used to generate our forms, has this already built-in. However, let's have a look at SeaSurf:

```
pip install flask-seasurf
```

With SeaSurf installed and using WTForms, it is now really easy to integrate it into our app. Open your app.py file and add the following:

```
from flask.ext.seasurf import SeaSurf
csrf = SeaSurf(app)
```

This simply enables SeaSurf for your app. Now, to enable the CSRF in your forms, open forms.py and create the following Mixin:

```
from flask.ext.wtf import HiddenField
import g

from app import app

class CSRFMixin(object):
    @staticmethod
    @app.before_request
    def add_csrf():
        self._csrf_token = HiddenField(default=g._csrf_token)
```

The preceding code creates a simple CSRF Mixin that can be used optionally within all your forms. The decorators ensure that the method is run before a request, in order to add the HiddenField field to your forms with the value of the randomly generated CSRF token. To use this Mixin in your forms, in this instance your login form, update the class as follows:

```
class LoginForm(Form, CSRFMixin):
```

That's it. We need to make this change for all the forms we want to protect, which is usually all of them.

# Creating Atom feeds

A really useful feature for any blog is to have the ability for your readers to keep up-to-date with the latest content. This most commonly happens with an RSS reader client that polls your RSS subscription feed. While RSS is widely used, a better, more mature subscription format is available and is called Atom.

Both are files that can be requested by a client, and are standard and simple XML data structures. Fortunately, an Atom feed generator is built into Flask; or, more specifically, a contributed module is built into the WSGI interface that Flask uses called Werkzeug.

Getting it up-and-running is simple, all we need to do is to get hold of our most recently published posts from the database. It may be best to create a new Blueprint for this; however, you can also do it within your `main.py`. We just need to make use of a few more modules:

```
from urlparse import urljoin
from flask import request, url_for
from werkzeug.contrib.atom import AtomFeed
from models import Entry
```

And create a new route:

```
@app.route('/latest.atom')
def recent_feed():
    feed = AtomFeed(
        'Latest Blog Posts',
        feed_url=request.url,
        url=request.url_root,
        author=request.url_root
    )
    entries = EntrY.query.filter(Entry.status ==
Entry.STATUS_PUBLIC).order_by(EntrY.created_timestamp.desc()).li
mit(15).all()
    for entry in entries:
        feed.add(
            entry.title,
            entry.body,
            content_type='html',
            url=urljoin(request.url_root, url_for("entries.detail",
slug=entry.slug) ),
            updated=entry.modified_timestamp,
            published=entry.created_timestamp
        )
    return feed.get_response()
```

Now run your Flask app and the Atom feed will be accessible from `http://127.0.0.1:5000/latest.atom`

# Syntax highlighting using Pygments

Often, as coders, we want to be able to display code in a web page, and while it is a skill to read that code without syntax highlighting, a few colors can make the reading experience much more pleasant.

As is always the way with Python, there is a module already available that is able to do that for you, and of course it can be installed easily by the following command:

`pip install Pygments`

> Pygments only works with the known sections of code. So, if you want to display code snippets, we can do that. If, however, you want to highlight inline sections of the code, we either follow the next section on Markdown, or we need to use some online Javascript such as `highlight.js`.

To create code snippets, we need to first create a new blueprint. Let's create a directory called `snippets`, then an `__init__.py` file, followed by a `blueprint.py` file with the following code:

```python
from flask import Blueprint, request, render_template, redirect, url_
for
from helpers import object_list
from app import db, app

from models import Snippet
from forms import SnippetForm

from pygments import highlight
from pygments.lexers import PythonLexer
from pygments.formatters import HtmlFormatter

snippets = Blueprint('snippets', __name__,
template_folder='templates')

@app.template_filter('pygments')
def pygments_filter(code):
    return highlight(code, PythonLexer(), HtmlFormatter())

@snippets.route('/')
def index():
    snippets =
Snippet.query.order_by(Snippet.created_timestamp.desc())
```

```
    return object_list('entries/index.html', snippets)

@snippets.route('/<slug>/')
def detail(slug):
    snippet = Snippet.query.filter(Snippet .slug ==
slug).first_or_404()
    return render_template('snippets/detail.html',
entry=snippet)

@snippets.route('/create/', methods=['GET', 'POST'])
def create():
    if request.method == 'POST':
        form = SnippetForm(request.form)
        if form.validate():
            snippet = form.save_entry(Snippet())
            db.session.add(snippet)
            db.session.commit()
            return redirect(url_for('snippets.detail',
slug=snippet.slug))
    else:
        form = SnippetForm()

    return render_template('snippets/create.html', form=form)

@snippets.route('/<slug>/edit/', methods=['GET', 'POST'])
def edit(slug):
    snippet = Snippet.query.filter(Snippet.slug ==
slug).first_or_404()
    if request.method == 'POST':
        form = SnippetForm(request.form, obj=snippet)
        if form.validate():
            snippet = form.save_entry(snippet)
            db.session.add(snippet)
            db.session.commit()
            return redirect(url_for('snippets.detail',
slug=entry.slug))
    else:
        form = EntryForm(obj=entry)

    return render_template('entries/edit.html', entry=snippet,
form=form)
```

In the preceding example, we set up the Pygments template filter that allows a string of code to be converted into HTML code. We also sneakily make use of the entries templates that are perfectly adequate for our needs. We use our own `detail.html` because that is where the magic happens with Pygments. We need to create a templates directory within the snippets director and another directory called snippets within templates, this is where we store our detail.html. So now our directory structure looks like app/snippets/templates/snipperts/detail.html Let's set up that file now, as follows:

```
{% extends "base.html" %}

{% block title %}{{ entry.title }} - Snippets{% endblock %}

{% block content_title %}Snippet{% endblock %}

{% block content %}
    {{ entry.body | pygments | safe}}
{% endblock %}
```

This is mostly identical to the `detail.html` that we used earlier in the book, except that we now pass it through the Pygments filter that we created in the app .As the template filter we used earlier produces raw HTML, we also need to mark its output as safe.

We also need to update our CSS file for the blog as Pygments uses CSS selectors to highlight words rather than wastefully writing the output to the page. It also allows us to modify the colors if we want. To find out what our CSS should be like, open up a Python shell and run the following commands:

```
>>> from pygments.formatters import HtmlFormatter
>>> print HtmlFormatter().get_style_defs('.highlight')
```

The preceding commands will now print out the example CSS that Pygments suggests and we can copy-and-paste it into our `.css` file in the `static` directory.

The rest of this code is not a great deal different from the previous Entry objects. It simply allows you to create, update, and view snippets. You will notice that we are using a `SnippetForm` here that we will define in a bit.

Also create a `models.py` with the following:

```
class Snippet(db.Model):
    STATUS_PUBLIC = 0
    STATUS_DRAFT = 1

    id = db.Column(db.Integer, primary_key=True)
    title = db.Column(db.String(100))
```

```
    slug = db.Column(db.String(100), unique=True)
    body = db.Column(db.Text)
    status = db.Column(db.SmallInteger, default=STATUS_PUBLIC)
    created_timestamp = db.Column(db.DateTime,
default=datetime.datetime.now)
    modified_timestamp = db.Column(
        db.DateTime,
        default=datetime.datetime.now,
        onupdate=datetime.datetime.now)

    def __init__(self, *args, **kwargs):
        super(Snippet, self).__init__(*args, **kwargs)  # Call
parent constructor.
        self.generate_slug()

    def generate_slug(self):
        self.slug = ''
        if self.title:
            self.slug = slugify(self.title)

    def __repr__(self):
        return '<Snippet: %s>' % self.title
```

Now we must re-run the `create_db.py` script to create the new table.

We will also need to create a new form so that the Snippets can be created. Within `forms.py,` add the following code:

```
from models import Snippet

class SnippetForm(wtforms.Form):
    title = wtforms.StringField('Title',
validators=[DataRequired()])
    body = wtforms.TextAreaField('Body',
validators=[DataRequired()])
    status = wtforms.SelectField(
        'Entry status',
        choices=(
            (Snippet.STATUS_PUBLIC, 'Public'),
            (Snippet.STATUS_DRAFT, 'Draft')),
        coerce=int)

    def save_entry(self, entry):
        self.populate_obj(entry)
        entry.generate_slug()
        return entry
```

Finally, we need to make sure that this blueprint is used by editing the `main.py` file and adding in the following:

```
from snippets.blueprint import snippets
app.register_blueprint(snippets, url_prefix='/snippets')
```

And, once we have added some code here using the `Snippet` model, the resulting code will render as shown in the following image:

```
class Snippet(db.Model):
    STATUS_PUBLIC = 0
    STATUS_DRAFT = 1

    id = db.Column(db.Integer, primary_key=True)
    title = db.Column(db.String(100))
    slug = db.Column(db.String(100), unique=True)
    body = db.Column(db.Text)
    status = db.Column(db.SmallInteger, default=STATUS_PUBLIC)
    created_timestamp = db.Column(db.DateTime, default=datetime.datetime.now)
    modified_timestamp = db.Column(
        db.DateTime,
        default=datetime.datetime.now,
        onupdate=datetime.datetime.now)

    def __init__(self, *args, **kwargs):
        super(Snippet, self).__init__(*args, **kwargs)  # Call parent constructor.
        self.generate_slug()

    def generate_slug(self):
        self.slug = ''
        if self.title:
            self.slug = slugify(self.title)

    def __repr__(self):
        return '<Snippet: %s>' % self.title
```

# Simple editing with Markdown

Markdown is a now widely used mark-up language on the web. It allows you to write plain text in a special format that can be programmatically converted to HTML. This can be especially useful when editing text from a mobile device where, for example, highlighting text to make it bold is significantly trickier than on a PC. You can see how to use the Markdown syntax at `http://daringfireball.net/projects/markdown/`

> One interesting thing to note with Markdown is that you can still use HTML as well as Markdown at the same time.

Of course, to get this running is quick and simple in Python. We install it as follows:

```
sudo pip install Flask-Markdown
```

Then we can apply it to our blueprint or app as follows:

```
from flaskext.markdown import Markdown
Markdown(app)
```

This makes a new filter available in our templates called `markdown` and that can be used when rendering your template:

```
{{ entry.body | markdown }}
```

Now all you need to do is write and save your blog entry content in Markdown.

As previously mentioned, you may also wish to prettify the code blocks; Markdown has this facility built-in, so we need to extend the previous example as follows:

```
from flaskext.markdown import Markdown
Markdown(app, extensions=['codehilite'])
```

This can now render the Markdown code blocks using Pygments. However, as Pygments uses CSS to add color to the code, we need to generate our CSS from Pygments. However, this time the parent block used has a class called `codehilite` (earlier it was called highlight), so we need to accommodate for this. In a Python shell, type the following:

```
>>> from pygments.formatters import HtmlFormatter
>>> print HtmlFormatter().get_style_defs('.codehilite')
```

Now add the output to your `.css` file in the `static` directory. So, with your included CSS, your Markdown entry could now look like this:

## Example Snippet Code

```
class Snippet(db.Model):
    STATUS_PUBLIC = 0
    STATUS_DRAFT = 1

    id = db.Column(db.Integer, primary_key=True)
    title = db.Column(db.String(100))
    slug = db.Column(db.String(100), unique=True)
    body = db.Column(db.Text)
    status = db.Column(db.SmallInteger, default=STATUS_PUBLIC)
    created_timestamp = db.Column(db.DateTime, default=datetime.datetime.now)
    modified_timestamp = db.Column(
        db.DateTime,
        default=datetime.datetime.now,
        onupdate=datetime.datetime.now)

    def __init__(self, *args, **kwargs):
        super(Snippet, self).__init__(*args, **kwargs)  # Call parent constructor.
        self.generate_slug()

    def generate_slug(self):
        self.slug = ''
        if self.title:
            self.slug = slugify(self.title)

    def __repr__(self):
        return '<Snippet: %s>' % self.title
```

Note that body here contains the code but is called body so that we can reuse some templates.

There are lots of other Markdown extensions built-in that we could also use; you can check them out and just use their name as a string when initializing the Markdown object.

# Caching with Flask-Cache and Redis

Sometimes, (and I know it's hard to imagine) we put a lot of effort into our sites, building in and adding features, and often that means we end up having to do a lot of database calls or complex template rendering for a page that is simply a static blog entry. Now database calls should not be slow and a lot of template renderings should not be noticeable but, if you expand that to lots of users (which hopefully you are expecting), this may become an issue.

So, if the site is mostly static why not store your response in a single, high-speed memory-based data store? No need for expensive database calls or complex template renderings; for the same input, or path, get the same content, and faster.

As is becoming a kind of a catch-phrase by now, we can already do this in Python and it is as simple as the following:

```
sudo pip install Flask-Cache
```

To get it running, add this to your app or your blueprint:

```
from flask.ext.cache import Cache

app = Flask(__name__)
cache = Cache(app, config={'CACHE_TYPE': 'redis'})
```

You will also want to install Redis of course, this can be done on Debian and Ubuntu systems quite simply:

**`sudo apt-get install redis-server`**

Unfortunately, Redis is not yet available in the Red Hat and CentOS packaging system. You can, however, download and compile Redis from their site at

`http://redis.io/download`

By default, Redis is unsecured; as long as we don't expose it to our network this should be fine and we do not need any more configuration for Flask-Cache. If, however, you are looking to lock it down, check out the Flask-Cache configuration for Redis.

Now we can use caching in our views (as well as any methods). This is as simple as using a decorator on a route. So, open a view and add the following:

```
@app.route("/")
@cache.cached(timeout=600) # 10 minutes
def homepage():
    ...
```

You will see here that the cached decorator is within the route and that we have a timeout value of 10 minutes, in seconds. This means that, however heavy the rendering of your homepage is, and however many database calls it may make, the response is going to be straight out of memory for that time period.

Obviously, caching has a time and a place and can be quite an art. If you have a custom homepage for each user, then caching will be useless. However, what we can do is cache sections of our template, so common areas such as all the <link> elements in the <head> will very rarely change but the url_for('static', ...) filter doesn't have to be regenerated each time. Look at the following code for example:

```
{% cache 1800 %}
<link rel="stylesheet" href="{{ url_for('static',
filename='css/blog.min.css') }}">
{% endcache %}
```

The preceding code section says that the link element should be cached for 30 minutes, in seconds. You may also want to do this for your references to the scripts as well. We could also use it for loading a list of the latest blog posts, for example.

# Creating secure, stable versions of your site by creating static content

One technique for a high-volume site with low-dynamic content is to create a site that is simply a static copy of the dynamic site. This works great for blogs as the content is generally static and updated, at the most, a couple of times a day. However, you are still doing a bunch of database calls and template renderings for the content that effectively doesn't change.

And, of course, there is a Flask extension that has this covered: Frozen-Flask. Frozen-Flask identifies the URLs in your Flask app and generates the content that should be there.

So, for the pages it generates the HTML and, for static content such as JavaScript and images, it pulls them out into a base directory that is a static copy of your site and that can be served up by your web server as static content.

This has the added benefit of the site being much more secure since the *active* version of the site cannot be changed by using the Flask app or the web server.

There are some drawbacks to this, of course. If you have dynamic content on your site—for example, comments—it is no longer possible to store and render them in the conventional way. Also, if you have multiple authors on your site, you need a way of sharing your database content so they don't end up producing separate copies of the site. Solutions are suggested at the end of this section. But first, let us install Frozen-Flask as follows:

```
pip install Frozen-Flask
```

Next we will need to create a file called `freeze.py`. This is a simple script that automatically sets up Frozen-Flask:

```
from flask_frozen import Freezer
from main import app

freezer = Freezer(app)

if __name__ == '__main__':
    freezer.freeze()
```

The above code uses all the defaults of Frozen-Flask and when run as follows:

```
python freeze.py
```

will create (or overwrite) the directory `build` that contains the static copy of your blog.

Frozen-Flask is quite smart and will automatically find all your links, as long as they are hierarchically referenced from the root homepage; for blog posts this works quite well. However, if entries get dropped from your homepage and they are accessed by an archive page on another URL, you may need to give Frozen-Flask pointers as to where to find those. For example, add the following to the `freeze.py` file:

```
import models


@freezer.register_generator
def archive():
    for post in models.Entry.all():
        yield {'detail': product.id}
```

Frozen-Flask is smart and uses the `url_for` method provided by Flask to create the static files. This means that anything that is available to the `url_for` method is available to be used by Frozen-Flask, if it cannot be found through the normal route.

# Commenting on a static site

So, as you might have guessed, by creating a static site you lose out on some blogging fundamentals—the one area that encourages communication and debate. Fortunately, there is a simple solution.

Blog comment hosting services such as Disqus and Discourse work much like a forum, with the exception that each topic is created by each blog post. You can use their services for free to run your discussion or, with Discourse, you can run their server on your own platform for free, as it is completely open source.

# Synchronizing multiple editors

Another issue with Frozen-Flask, one that a person running the blog won't notice, is this: with multiple authors spread across a network, how do you manage the database where your posts are stored? Everyone will need the same up-to-date copy of the database; otherwise, when you generate the static copy of the site, it won't be able to create all the content.

If you all work in the same environment, one solution is to have a working copy of the blog running on a server within the network and, when it comes to publishing time, it will use that centralized database to create the published version of the blog.

If, however, you all work in disparate locations where a centralized database is not ideal or impossible to secure, the other solution is to use a file-system based database engine such as SQLite. Then, when an update is made to the database, that file can be spread to others via e-mail, Dropbox, Skype, and so on. They then have an up-to-date copy of the database that they can locally run Frozen-Flask from to create the publishable content.

# Asynchronous tasks with Celery

Celery is a library that allows you to run asynchronous tasks within Python. This is especially helpful in Python as Python runs single threaded and you may find that you have a long-running task that you wish to either start and discard; or you may wish to give the user of your website some feedback on the progress of the said task.

One such example is e-mail. A user may request an e-mail to be sent, for example a password reset request, and you don't want them waiting for the page to load while the e-mail is generated and sent. We can set this up as a start and discard operation and let the user know that the request is being dealt with.

The way Celery is able to escape the single-threaded environment of Python is that we have to run a Celery broker instance separately which; this creates what Celery calls workers that do the actual work. Your Flask app and the workers then communicate with each other via the messaging broker.

So obviously, we need to install Celery and I'm sure you can guess by now that the command you need is the following one:

```
pip install celery
```

Now we need a message broker server. There are plenty to choose from; check out Celery's website for the supported ones, but, however, since we have already set up Redis in the Flask-Cache setup, let's use that.

Now we need to tell Celery how to use the Redis server. Open up the Flask app configuration file and add the following line:

```
CELERY_BROKER_URL = 'redis://localhost:6379/0'
```

This configuration tells your instance of Celery where to find the message broker that it needs to communicate with the Celery broker. Now we need to initialize the Celery instance in our app. In the `main.py file`, add the following:

```
from celery import Celery

celery = Celery(app.name, broker=app.config['CELERY_BROKER_URL'])
```

This creates an instance of `Celery` with configuration from the Flask configuration file so we can also access the `celery` object from the Celery broker and share the same setup.

Now we need something for the Celery worker processes to do. At this point, we are going to make use of the Flask-Mail library:

**pip install Flask-Mail**

We are also going to need some configuration for this to run. Add the following parameters to your Flask configuration file:

```
MAIL_SERVER = "example.com"
MAIL_PORT = 25
MAIL_USERNAME = "email_username"
MAIL_PASSWORD = "email_password"
```

This configuration tells Flask-Mail where your e-mail server is. It is likely that the defaults may be good enough for you, or you may need more options. Check out the Flask-Mail configuration for more options.

Now lets create a new file called `tasks.py` and create some tasks to run as follows:

```
from flask_mail import Mail, Message
from main import app, celery

mail = Mail(app)

@celery.task
def send_password_verification(email, verification_code):
  msg = Message(
    "Your password reset verification code is:
{0}".format(verification_code),
               sender="from@example.com",
               recipients=[email]
  )
  mail.send(msg)
```

This is a really simple message generation; we are just generating an e-mail message with the content saying what the new password is, where the e-mail is from (our mail server), who the e-mail is going to, and the e-mail address of the user whose account it supposedly is, and then sends; the message is then sent via the already set up mail instance.

Now we need to get our Flask app to make use of the new asynchronous ability. Let's create a view that listens for an e-mail address being POSTed to it. This could be in any of the blueprints to do with accounts or your main app.

```
import tasks

@app.route("/reset-password", methods=['POST'])
def reset_password():
  user_email = request.form.get('email')
  user = db.User.query.filter(email=user_email).first()
  if user:
    new_password = db.User.make_password("imawally")
    user.update({"password_hash": new_password})
    user.commit()
    tasks.send_password_verification.delay(user.email,
new_password)
    flash("Verification e-mail sent")
  else:
    flash("User not found.")
  redirect(url_for('homepage'))
```

The preceding view accepts a POSTed message from a browser that contains the e-mail of the user who is is claiming to have forgotten his password. We first look up the user by their e-mail address to see if the user does indeed exist in our database. Obviously, there's no point resetting the password on an account that doesn't exist. Of course, if they don't exist, the user will be given a message accordingly.

However, if the user account does exist, the first thing to do is to generate them a new password. We use a hard-coded example password here. That password is then updated in the database so that the user can use it to log in when they receive the e-mail. Once all of that is out of the way, we then run .delay on the task we created earlier with the arguments that we want to use. This instructs Celery to run the underlying method when it is ready.

Note that this is not the best solution for doing password resets. It is just to illustrate how you may want to do it in a succinct way. Password rests are a surprisingly complicated area and there are lots of things you can do to improve the security and privacy of this facility such as checking the CSRF value, limiting how many times the method is called, and using a randomly generated URL for users to reset their passwords at rather than a hard-coded solution that is sent via e-mail.

Finally, we need to run the Celery broker when we run our Flask app; otherwise, very little is going to happen. Don't forget, this broker is the process that starts all our asynchronous workers. The simplest thing we can do is run the following command from within your Flask app directory:

```
celeryd -A main worker
```

This quite simply starts the Celery broker and tells it to look for the celery configuration within the main app so that it can find the configuration and the tasks it is supposed to be running.

Now we can start our Flask app and send some e-mails.

# Creating command line instructions with Flask-script

One really useful thing to do with Flask is to create a command-line interface so that, when others use your software, they can easily make use of the methods you provide, such as setting up the database, creating administrative users, or updating the CSRF secret key.

One area where we already have a script resembling this and one that can be used in this way is the create_db.py script in *Chapter 2*, *Relational Databases with SQLAlchemy*. To do this, there is again, a Flask extension. Just run the following command:

```
pip install Flask-Script
```

Now the interesting thing with Flask-Script is that the commands work a lot like the routes and views in Flask. Let's look at an example:

```
from flask.ext.script import Manager
from main import app

manager = Manager(app)
```

```
@manager.command
def hello():
    print "Hello World"

if __name__ == "__main__":
    manager.run()
```

You can see here that Flask-Script refers to itself as Manager, but that the manager also hooks itself into the Flask app. This means you can do anything with the Flask app just by using the `app` reference.

So, if we convert our `create_db.py` app into a Flask-Script app, we should create a file for this to work in. Let's call it `manage.py` and insert from the file `create_db.py`:

```
from main import db

@manager.command
def create_db():
    db.create_all()
```

All this does is set up a decorator so that the `manage.py` with the argument `create_db` will run the method which was in `create_db.py`.

We can now run from the following command line:

```
python manage.py create_db
```

# References

- https://highlightjs.org/
- http://pythonhosted.org/Flask-Markdown/
- http://daringfireball.net/projects/markdown/
- http://pythonhosted.org/Markdown/extensions
- https://pythonhosted.org/Frozen-Flask/
- https://disqus.com/
- http://www.discourse.org
- http://eviltrout.com/2014/01/22/embedding-discourse.html
- http://flask-script.readthedocs.org/en/latest/
- https://pythonhosted.org/Flask-Mail/

# Summary

In this chapter, we have done a wide variety of things. You have seen how to create your own Markdown renderer, so editing becomes easier, and move commands so they are within Flask and more manageable. We have created Atom feeds so that our readers can find new content when it is posted, and created asynchronous tasks so that we don't lock up the user's browser while waiting for a page to load.

In our final chapter, we will learn how to turn our simple application into a fully deployed blog that has all the features discussed, secured, and ready to use.

# 10
# Deploying Your Application

In this chapter, we will learn how to deploy our Flask applications securely and in an automated, repeatable manner. We will see how to configure commonly used **WSGI (Web Server Gateway Interface)** capable servers such as Apache, Nginx, as well as the Python Webserver Gunicorn. Then we will see how to secure a part or the entire site using SSL, before finally wrapping up our application in a configuration management tool to automate our deployment.

In this chapter we shall learn the following topics:

- Configuring commonly-used WSGI servers
- Serving static files efficiently
- Using SSL to secure your site
- Automating deployment using Ansible

## Running Flask with a WSGI server

It is important to note that Flask, by itself, is not a web server. Web servers are tools that are Internet-facing, have had many years of development and patching applied to them, and can run many services at once.

Running Flask by itself as a Web server on the Internet will most likely be fine, thanks to the Werkzeug WSGI layer However, the real focus of development on Flask is page-routing and rendering the system. Running Flask as a web server may have unintended effects. Ideally, Flask will sit behind a web server and be called upon when the server recognizes a request for your app. To do this, the web server and Flask need to be able to speak the same language.

Fortunately the Werkzeug stack, upon which Flask is built, is designed to speak WSGI. WSGI is a common protocol used by web servers such as Apache's httpd and Nginx. It can be used to manage the load on your Flask app and communicate the important bits of information about where the requests came from and what kind of headers the request has, all in a way that Python can understand.

However, to get Werkzeug to talk to your web server using the WSGI protocol, we must use a gateway. This will take the requests from your web server and the Python application and translate the actions between them. Most web servers will speak WSGI although some need a module, and some a separate gateway such as uWSGI.

One of the first things to do is to create a WSGI file for the WSGI gateway to communicate through. This is simply a Python file with a known structure so that the WSGI gateway can access it. We need to create a file called `wsgi.py` in the same directory as the rest of your blog app and it will contain:

```
from app import app as application
```

Flask, by default, is WSGI-compatible so we just need to declare the object in the right way for the WSGI gateway to understand. Now the web server needs to be configured to find this file.

# Apache's httpd

Apache's httpd is probably the most widely used web server on the internet right now. The program's name is actually httpd, and it is maintained by the Apache Software Foundation. However, most people refer to it as *Apache* so that is what we shall call it as well.

To make sure that Apache and the WSGI module are installed on Debian- and Ubuntu-based systems, run the following command:

```
sudo apt-get install apache2 libapache2-mod-wsgi
```

However, on Red Hat- and Fedora-based systems run the following command:

```
sudo yum install httpd mod_wsgi
```

To set up the Apache configuration, we must create a configuration file that will specify a new VirtualHost. You must locate the directory on your system where these files are kept. In Debian-based systems, such as Ubuntu, this will be in `/etc/apache2/sites-available`; create your `blog` file in there. On Red Hat/Fedora-based systems, we need to create a file called `blog.conf` in the `/etc/apache2/conf.d` directory.

In that configuration file, update the content with the following code:

```
<VirtualHost *:80>

    WSGIScriptAlias / <path to app>/wsgi.py

    <Directory <path to app>/>
        Order deny,allow
        Allow from all
    </Directory>

</VirtualHost>
```

This configuration instructs Apache that, for every request to the host on port `80`, there is to attempt to load from the `wsgi.py` script. The directory section tells Apache how to handle requests to that directory and, by default, it is best to deny access to the files within your source directory to anyone accessing the web server. Be aware that, in this instance, `<path to app>` is the full absolute path to the directory where the `wsgi.py` file is stored.

We will now need to enable the WSGI module for Apache's httpd server. This is so that Apache knows to use it when specifying the WSGI configuration. On Debian- and Ubuntu-based systems, we just run this command:

**sudo a2enmod wsgi**

However on Red Hat and CentOS systems, it is a little more tricky. We will need to create or modify the file `/etc/httpd/conf.d/wsgi.conf` to contain the following line:

```
LoadModule wsgi_module modules/mod_wsgi.so
```

Now we need to enable our new site on the web server on Debian- and Ubuntu-based systems by running this:

**sudo a2ensite blog**

This instructs Apache to create a symbolic link from `/etc/apache2/sites-available` to `/etc/apache2/sites-enabled`, where Apache actually gets its configuration from. Now we need to restart Apache. This can be performed in many ways in your particular environment or distribution. The simplest may be just to run the following command:

**sudo service apache2 restart**

So all we need to do is connect to the web server through your browser by going to `http://localhost/`.

Check for any issues in your `/var/log/apache2/error.log` in Debian and Ubuntu systems and `/var/log/httpd/error_log` in Red Hat- and CentOS-based systems.

Be aware that some Linux distros ship with a default configuration that must be disabled. This can likely be disabled in Debian- and Ubuntu-based systems by typing the following command:

```
sudo a2dissite default
```

However, in Red Hat- and CentOS-based systems we need to remove the `/etc/httpd/conf.d/welcome.conf` file:

```
sudo rm /etc/httpd/conf.d/welcome.conf
```

We will, of course, have to restart the server again for Debian- and Ubuntu-based systems:

```
sudo service apache2 restart
```

And in Red Hat- and CentOS-based systems:

```
sudo service httpd restart
```

Apache also has a reload option rather than restart. This tells the server to have a look at the configuration files again and work with them. This is typically faster than restart and can keep the existing connections open. Where as, restart exits the server and starts again, taking open connections with it. The benefit of restart is that it is more definitive and, for setup purposes, more consistent.

## Serving static files

One very important step to go through when using Flask, through a web server, is to decrease the load on your app by creating a shortcut for your web server to the static content on your site. This offloads to the web server the relatively trivial task of serving basic files to the end browser, making the process faster and more responsive. It is also a straightforward thing to do.

Edit your `blog.conf` file to add the following line within the `<VirtualHost *:80>` tags:

```
Alias /static <path to app>/static
```

Here, `<path to app>` is the full absolute path to the directory where your static directory exists. Then reload the Apache configuration for Debian- and Ubuntu-based systems as follows:

`sudo service apache2 restart`

And for Red Hat- and CentOS-based systems as follows:

`sudo service httpd restart`

This will now inform Apache where to look for files when `/static` is requested by the browser. You will be able to see this happening by looking at your Apache log file, `/var/log/apache2/access.log` for Debian- and Ubuntu-based systems and `/var/log/httpd/access.log` for Red Hat- and CentOS-based systems.

# Nginx

Nginx is rapidly becoming the de facto web server to replace Apache's httpd. It is proven to be faster and more lightweight and its configuration, although quite different, can be simpler to understand.

While Nginx has supported WSGI for some time, even newer Linux distros may not have updated to it and therefore we must use an interface layer called **uWSGI** to access the Python web apps. uWSGI is a WSGI gateway written in Python that can translate between WSGI and your web server via sockets. We need to install both Nginx and uWSGI. In Debian and Ubuntu based systems run the following:

`sudo apt-get install nginx`

And in Red Hat- or Fedora-based systems, the following

`sudo yum install nginx`

Now since uWSGI is a Python module, we can install it using `pip`:

`sudo pip install uwsgi`

To configure Nginx in Debian- and Ubuntu-based systems, create a file called `blog.conf` in `/etc/nginx/sites-available` or, in Red Hat- or Fedora-based systems, create the file in `/etc/nginx/conf.d` and add the content with:

```
server {
    listen      80;
    server_name _;

    location / { try_files $uri @blogapp; }
```

```
        location @blogapp {
            include uwsgi_params;
            uwsgi_pass unix:/var/run/blog.wsgi.sock;
        }
    }
```

This configuration is very much the same as the Apache configuration, although expressed in Nginx form. It accepts connections on port 80 and for any server name, it tries to access the blog.wsgi.sock, which is a unix socket file used to communicate with uWSGI. You will notice that @blogapp is used as a shortcut reference to the location.

Only in Debian- and Ubuntu-based systems do we now need to enable the new site, by creating a symlink from the available site to the enabled one:

```
sudo ln -s /etc/nginx/sites-available/blog.conf /etc/nginx/sites-enabled
```

Then we need to tell uWSGI where to find the socket file so it can communicate with Nginx. To do this, we need to create a uWSGI configuration file in the blog app directory called uwsgi.ini that contains the following:

```
[uwsgi]
base = <path to app>
app = app
module = app
socket = /var/run/blog.wsgi.sock
```

You will have to change <path to app> to the path where your app.py file exists. Also note how the socket is set up in the same path as specified in the Nginx site configuration file.

> You may note that the formatting and structure of the INI file are very much like a Windows INI file.

We can verify if this configuration works by running the following command:

```
uwsgi -ini uwsgi.ini
```

Now Nginx knows how to talk to the gateway but isn't yet using the site configuration file; we need to restart it. This can be performed in many ways in your particular environment. The simplest may be just to run the following command:

```
sudo service nginx restart
```

So all we need to do is connect to the web server through your browser by going to `http://localhost/`.

Be aware that some Linux distros ship with a default configuration that must be disabled. This can normally be done in both Debian- and Ubuntu-based systems, and Red Hat- and CentOS-based systems, by deleting the `/etc/nginx/conf.d/default.conf` file.

```
sudo rm /etc/nginx/conf.d/default.conf
```

And restarting the `nginx` service:

```
sudo service nginx restart
```

> Nginx also has a reload option rather than restart. This tells the server to have a look at the configuration files again and work with them. This is typically faster than restart and can keep existing connections open. Where as, restart exits the server and starts again, taking open connections with it. The benefit of restart is that it is more definitive and, for setup purposes, more consistent.

## Serving static files

One very important step to go through when using Flask, through a web server, is to decrease the load on your app by creating a shortcut for your web server to the static content on your site. This offloads, to the web server, the relatively trivial task of serving basic files to the end browser, making the process faster and more responsive. It is also a straightforward task to do.

Edit your `blog.conf` file to add this line within the server { tag:

```
location /static {
    root <path to app>/static;
}
```

where <path to app> is the full absolute path to the directory where your static directory exists. Reload the Nginx configuration:

```
sudo service nginx restart
```

This will now inform Nginx where to look for files when /static is requested by the browser. You will be able to see this happening by looking at your Nginx log file, /var/log/nginx/access.log.

# Gunicorn

Gunicorn is a web server written in Python. It already understands WSGI and so does Flask, so getting Gunicorn running it is as easy as entering the following code:

```
pip install gunicorn
gunicorn app:app
```

where app:app is your app and the module name the one we used within that (much the same as the uWSGI configuration). There are way more options than that, but it is useful, for example, to work from and set a port and binding:

```
gunicorn --bind 127.0.0.1:8000 app:app
```

The --bind flag tells Gunicorn what interface to connect to and on what port. This is useful if we need to only use the web app internally.

Another useful flag is the --daemon flag that tells Gunicorn to run in the background and detach from your shell. This means we no longer have direct control of the process but it is running and can be accessed via the bind interface and the port that was setup.

# Securing your site with SSL

In an increasingly ruthless Internet, it is important to improve the security of your site by proving its authenticity. A common tool for improving this for your site is to use SSL, or even better TLS.

SSL and TLS certificates allow your server to be verified by a trusted third-party based upon the domain name that your browser is connecting to. This means that, as a web user, we can be sure that the web site we are talking to hasn't been changed in transit, is the correct server we are talking to, and that the data being sent between the server and our browser cannot be sniffed. This obviously becomes important when we want to verify that the information our users are sending us is valid, and protected, and our users want to know that our data is protected in transit.

# Getting your certificate

The first thing to do is generate your SSL certificate request. This is used in conjunction with a third party who signs the request to verify your server with any browser. There are a few ways of doing this, depending on your system, but the easiest is to run the command:

```
openssl req -nodes -newkey rsa:2048 -sha256 -keyout private.key -out
public.csr
```

You will now be asked a few questions about the organization you're affiliated to, but the important line is the Common Name. This is the domain name (without `https://`) that your server will be accessed at:

```
Country Name (2 letter code) [AU]: GB
State or Province Name (full name) [Some-State]: London
Locality Name (eg, city) []: London
Organization Name (eg, company) [Internet Widgits Pty Ltd]:
Example Company
Organizational Unit Name (eg, section) []: IT
Common Name (eg, YOUR name) []: blog.example.com
Email Address []:
A challenge password []:
An optional company name []:
```

You can see here we used `blog.example.com` as our example domain name that our blog app will be accessed at. You must use your own here. E-mail addresses and passwords are not hugely important and can be left blank, but you should fill in the `Organization Name` field as this will be the name your SSL certificate will be recognized as. If you are not a company, just use your own name.

That command generates two files for us; one is a `private.key` file, the file our server will use to sign our communication with the browser, and the other is `public.csr`, which is the certificate request file sent to the third-party service that handles the verification between the server and your browser.

> Public/Private key cryptography is a vast but well explored subject. In the light of the Heartbleed attack, it is worth having a reasonable understanding of this, if you are looking to secure a server.

The next step is to sign your `public.csr` request with a third party. There are many services that will do this for you, some free and some at a slight cost; some such as **Let's Encrypt** automate the entire process with a script completely free of cost. All of them offer essentially the same service, but they may not all be built-in to all browsers, and offer various levels of support for varying degrees of cost.

These services will go through a verification process with you, ask for your `public.csr` certificate request, and return you a signed `.crt` certificate file for your host name.

> Note that it will most likely help you to name your `.crt` and `.key` file with your site's host name in it, with which you applied for the certificate. In our case, this would be `blog.example.com.crt`.

Your new `.crt` file and your existing `.key` file can be placed anywhere on your server. However, typically the `.crt` files go into `/etc/ssl/certs` and the `.key` files in `/etc/ssl/private`.

With all the correct files in the right place, we need to reopen the existing Apache configuration that we used for our blog service. It would be preferable to run a normal HTTP and HTTPS service. However, since we have gone to the effort of setting up the HTTPS service, it makes sense to enforce it by redirecting our users. This can be done using a new specification called HSTS however not all builds of web servers support this yet, so we will use rewrites.

> You can run tests on your local machine with SSL certs by adding an entry to your operating system's host file for your domain. Just don't forget to remove it when you are done.

# Apache httpd

The first thing to change is the port on the `VirtualHost` line from the default HTTP port of `80` to the default HTTPS port of `443`:

```
<VirtualHost *:443>
```

We should also specify the server's hostname the SSL cert is being used on; so within the VirtualHost section add a `ServerName` parameter. This will ensure the certificate will not be used in the wrong domain.

```
ServerName blog.example.com
```

You must replace `blog.example.com` with the host name that you will be using.

We also need to set up the SSL configuration so as to tell Apache how to respond:

```
SSLEngine on
SSLProtocol -all +TLSv1 +SSLv2
SSLCertificateFile /etc/ssl/certs/blog.example.com.crt
SSLCertificateKeyFile /etc/ssl/private/blog.example.com.key
SSLVerifyClient None
```

What is going on here is that the SSL module in Apache is being enabled, the public certificate and private key file are being specified for this site, and there is no client certificate required. It is important to disable the default SSL protocols and enable TLS, which is considered more secure than SSL. However, SSLv2 is still enabled to support older browsers.

Now we need to test it. Let's restart Apache:

**`sudo service apache2 restart`**

Try connecting to the web server with your browser, not forgetting that you are now using `https://`.

Now that is working, the final step is to redirect plain old HTTP to HTTPS. In the configuration file, again add the following:

```
<VirtualHost *:80>
  ServerName blog.example.com
  RewriteEngine On
  RewriteRule (.*) https://%{HTTP_HOST}%{REQUEST_URI}
</VirtualHost>
```

We create a new `VirtualHost` for port `80` and specify that it is for the `ServerName` `blog.example.com` hostname. But then we use the `Rewrite` module in Apache to simply redirect the browser to the same URL it requested, however, using HTTPS at the beginning.

Again, restart Apache:

**`sudo service apache2 restart`**

Now test this configuration in your browser on the site; verify that you get redirected to HTTPS for whichever page you access.

# Nginx

The configuration of Nginx is pretty simple. In much the same way as the Apache configuration, we need to change the port that Nginx will be listening to for our site. Since HTTPS works on port 443, the difference here is to tell Nginx to expect SSL connections. In the configuration, we must update the line as follows:

```
listen    443 ssl;
```

Now to add the SSL configuration to the server element of the configuration, enter the following:

```
server_name blog.example.com;
ssl_certificate /etc/ssl/certs/blog.example.com.crt;
ssl_certificate_key /etc/ssl/private/blog.example.com.key;
ssl_protocols TLSv1 SSLv2;
```

This tells Nginx to apply this configuration to requests for the blog.example.com hostname (don't forget to replace it with your own), as we wouldn't like to send the SSL cert for a domain that it doesn't apply to. We also specify the public certificate file location and the private SSL key file location on the file system. Finally, we specify the SSL protocols we want to use, which means enabling TLS (considered more secure than SSL). However SSLv2 is still enabled to support older browsers.

Now to test it. Let's restart the Nginx service:

**sudo service nginx restart**

Try connecting to the web server with your browser, not forgetting you are now using https://.

Once we have proved that it is working, the final step is to redirect plain old HTTP to HTTPS. In the configuration file again add the following:

```
server {
    listen 80;
    server_name blog.example.com;
    rewrite ^ https://$server_name$request_uri? permanent;
}
```

This works much the same as the previous, plain old HTTP configuration; except that we use the rewrite command to tell Nginx to pick up all URLs and send a redirect command to the browser accessing port HTTP to go to HTTPS instead, with the exact path they attempted to use on HTTP.

For the last time, restart Nginx:

```
sudo service nginx restart
```

Finally, test your browser on the site on which you get redirected to HTTPS whichever page you access.

# Gunicorn

Gunicorn has also had SSL support added to it as of 0.17. To enable SSL from the command line, we need a few flags:

```
gunicorn --bind 0.0.0.0:443 --certfile /etc/ssl/certs/blog.example.
com.crt --keyfile /etc/ssl/private/blog.example.com.key --ssl-version 2
--ciphers TLSv1  app:app
```

This works much the same as the Nginx and Apache SSL configurations. It specifies the port to bind to, as well as all the interfaces in this case. It then directs Gunicorn to the public certificate and private key files, and opts to use SSLv2 for older browsers and the (commonly considered more secure) TLS cipher protocols.

Test this in your browser by going to the host name and the HTTPS in your browser.

Now that is ready, let's set up a redirection from port 80 to port 443. This is quite complicated in Gunicorn as it does not have a built-in redirection facility. One solution is to create a really simple Flask app that is started on port 80 in Gunicorn and redirects to port 443. It would be a new app with a new app.py file, and with its contents looking as follows:

```
from flask import Flask,request, redirect
import urlparse

app = Flask(__name__)

@app.route('/')
@app.route('/<path:path>')
def https_redirect(path='/'):
    url = urlparse.urlunparse((
        'https',
        request.headers.get('Host'),
        path,
        '','',''
    ))

    return redirect(url, code=301)
```

```
if __name__ == '__main__':
    app.run()
```

This is a really simple Flask app that can be used anywhere to redirect a browser to the equivalent URL that was requested of it, but with HTTPS on the front. It builds a URL by making use of the standard Python `urlparse` library, the requested hostname using the header that is sent by the browser to the server, and the generic path variable in the route to pick up all document requests. It then uses the Flask `redirect` method to tell the browser where it really needs to go.

> Note that the empty strings are important to the urlunparse function as it is expecting a complete URL tuple, much like that generated by urlparse.

It is likely you will know how to run this in Gunicorn by now, nevertheless the command to use is as follows:

```
gunicorn --bind 0.0.0.0:80 app:app
```

Now connect using your browser to your old HTTP host and you should be redirected to the HTTPS version.

# Automating deployment using Ansible

Ansible is a configuration management tool. It allows us to automate the deployment of our applications in a repeatable and manageable manner, without having to consider how our application is deployed each time.

Ansible works both locally and over SSH. One of the clever things you can do with Ansible is to get Ansible to configure itself. Based on your own configuration, it can then be told to deploy the other machines that it needs.

We, however, are just going to concentrate on building our own local Flask instance using Apache, WSGI, and Flask.

The first thing to do is install Ansible on the machine that we are going to deploy our Flask app on to. Since Ansible is written in Python, we can achieve this quite simply by making use of `pip`:

```
sudo pip install ansible
```

We now have a configuration manager and, since a configuration manager is designed to set up servers, let's build up a playbook that Ansible can use to build the entire machine.

In a new project or directory, create a file called `blog.yml`. We are creating a file that Ansible calls a Playbook; it is a list of commands that will run in sequence and build our blog running under Apache. For simplicity, in this file it is assumed that you are using an Ubuntu-derivative operating system:

```
---

- hosts: webservers
  user: ubuntu
  sudo: True

  vars:
    app_src: ../blog
    app_dest: /srv/blog


  tasks:
    - name: install necessary packages
      action: apt pkg=$item state=installed
      with_items:
        - apache2
        - libapache2-mod-wsgi
        - python-setuptools
    - name: Enable wsgi module for Apache
      action: command a2enmod wsgi
    - name: Blog app configuration for Apache
      action: template src=templates/blog dest=/etc/apache/sites-
available/blog
    - name: Copy blog app in
      action: copy src=${app_src} dest=${app_dest}
    - name: Enable site
      action: command a2ensite blog
    - name: Reload Apache
      action: service name=apache2 state=reloaded
```

An Ansible Playbook is a YAML file that consists of a few sections; the main section describes the "play". The `hosts` value describes what group of machines the subsequent settings should apply to. `user` describes what user the play should run as; for you, this should be a user that Ansible can run as to install your application. The `sudo` setting tells Ansible to run this play with `sudo` permissions and not to run it as root.

The `vars` section describes variables common to the playbook. These settings can be found easily as they are at the top but can also be used later in the playbook configuration in the format `${example_variable}`, if `example_variable` was defined in the `vars` section here. The most important variable here is the `app_src` variable which tells Ansible where to find our app when it is copying it to the correct location. In this example, we are assuming it is in a directory called `blog`, but for you it may be located elsewhere on your file system and you may need to update this variable.

The final and most important section is the `tasks` section. This tells Ansible what to run when it is updating the machine it is controlling. If you are familiar with Ubuntu, these tasks should be somewhat familiar. `action: apt`, for example, tells apt to make sure that all the packages specified in the `with_items` list are installed. You will notice the `$item` variable with the `pkg` argument. The `$item` variable is automatically populated by Ansible as it iterates over the `with_items` command and the `apt` command uses the `pkg` argument to verify that the package is installed.

The subsequent tasks enable the WSGI module using the command-line command `a2enmod wsgi`, which is shorthand in Debian systems for enabling a module, setting up the Apache configuration for our blog site by populating a template. Fortunately for us, the language Ansible uses for its templates is Jinja, which you are most likely already familiar with. The contents of our template file should be relative to this `blog.yml`, in a directory called `templates`, and a file called `blog`. The contents should look like the following:

```
NameVirtualHost *:80

<VirtualHost *:80>
    WSGIScriptAlias / {{ app_dest }}/wsgi.py

    <Directory {{ app_dest }}/>
        Order deny,allow
        Allow from all
    </Directory>
</VirtualHost>
```

This should be pretty familiar, it is a direct rip-off of the example in the Apache section; however, we have made use of the Ansible variables to populate the locations of the blog app. This means that, if we want to install the app to another location, it will just be a matter of updating the `app_dest` variable.

Finally, among the Playbook tasks, it copies our all-important blog app onto the machine, enables the site in Apache by using the Debian shorthand, and reloads Apache so it can make use of the site.

So all that is left is to run Ansible on that machine and get it to build your system for you.

```
ansible-playbook blog.yml --connection=local
```

This tells Ansible to run the Playbook file `blog.yml` that we created earlier and to use it on the `local` connection type, which means applying to the local machine.

> **Ansible Tips**
>
> It is worth noting this may not be the best way to use Ansible in a large distributed environment. For one, you may want to apply it to remote machines or to separate out the Apache configuration, Apache WSGI configuration, Flask app configuration, and blog configuration into separate files that Ansible calls a role; this will make them reusable.
>
> Another useful tip would be to to specify the configuration file used and set up the static directory in Apache. Read the Ansible documentation for more ideas about ways to improve your deployment:
>
> `http://docs.ansible.com/`

# Read more

For more information on how to secure your Flask deployment more effectively in Apache and WSGI by creating shell-less users that can only run the Flask app, see `http://www.subdimension.co.uk/2012/04/24/Deploying_Flask_to_Apache.html`.

This guide has more examples for CentOS systems along with Lighttpd and Gunicorn all through Ansible `https://www.zufallsheld.de/2014/11/19/deploying-lighttpd-your-flask-apps-gunicorn-and-supervisor-with-ansible-on-centos/`.

# Summary

In this chapter, we have seen many ways in which you can run your Flask app, including securing it for privacy and security in multiple web servers and serving static files to reduce load on your Flask app. We have also made a configuration file for Ansible that will enable repeatable application deployment so that if the machine ever needs to be built again, it will be a simple task.

# Index

# M

**macros**
about 86
reference link 86
**Markdown**
about 15
URL 190
used, for editing 190-192
**mixins 143**
**mocking, objects 177-179**
**models**
about 26
Admin model forms, customizing 134, 135
exposing 126-129
filters, adding to list view 132-134
list views, customizing 129-131
search, adding to list view 132-134
slugs, generating 138-140
User form, enhancing 136, 137
**multiple editors**
synchronizing 195

# N

**negation 36**
**Nginx**
about 207, 208
static files, serving 209, 210
with SSL support 214

# O

**Object Relational Mapping (ORM) 23**
**objects**
mocking 177-179
**one() method**
versus first() method 34
**operator precedence 37**

# P

**pagination links**
adding 71, 72
**postprocessors**
using 160, 161
**preprocessors**
using 160, 161

**Pro Git**
about 16
URL 16
**Pygments**
used, for syntax highlighting 186-189
**Python's unit test module 168, 169**

# R

**Redis**
URL 193
used, for caching 192, 193
**relational database**
advantages 22

# S

**schema**
Flask-Migrate, adding 43, 44
initial migration, creating 44
modifying 43
schema migration, creating 149
status column, adding 45
**SeaSurf**
about 183
adding 184
**Secure Socket Layer (SSL) 14**
**sessions 120, 121**
**slugs**
generating 138-140
**SQLAlchemy**
about 22
benefits 23
connecting, to database 25, 26
database engine, selecting 25
installing 24
online resources 24
URL, for documentation 26, 42
using, in Flask app 24
**SSL**
certificate request, generating 211, 212
used, for securing site 210
with Apache httpd 212, 213
with Gunicorn 215, 216
with Nginx 214
**static assets**
managing, via Flask-Admin 140, 141

static files
serving 100
static site
commenting 195
creating 194
multiple editors, synchronizing 195
status column
adding, to schema 45
syntax highlighting
with Pygments 186-189

# T

tagging system
backrefs, using 42
building 37-40
tags, adding from entries 41
tags, removing from entries 41
tags
listing 68
modifying, on posts 94-96
saving, on posts 94-96
template, Flask-Admin
about 145
blocks 145
using 146
test-driven development (TDD) 169
testing configuration file
creating 176, 177
tests, Jinja2
about 54
URL 54
Traceback 13

# U

unit testing
about 167, 168
API, testing 175, 176
example 169-171
page, testing 173-175
Python's unit test module 168, 169
references 182
with Flask 171, 172

URL scheme
creating 60, 61
detail view, building 66
entries, listing for given tag 67
full-text search, adding 69, 70
index view, building 63, 64
purpose 61
structure 61
tags, listing 68
URL routes, defining 62
User form
enhancing 136, 137
user model
active field 104
created_timestamp field 104
creating 104, 105
email (unique) field 104
name field 104
password_hash field 104
slug field 104
user objects
creating 108, 109
user's drafts
displaying 119, 120
uWSGI 207

# V

validator 82
view
form, creating 77, 78
view access
author, setting on blog entries 117
delete view, protecting 118
edit view, protecting 117, 118
entry's author, storing 115, 116
restricting 114
user's drafts, displaying 119, 120

# W

Web Server Gateway Interface (WSGI)
server
Apache httpd 204-206
Flask, running 203, 204
Nginx 207, 208

**Thank you for buying**
# Learning Flask Framework

## About Packt Publishing

Packt, pronounced 'packed', published its first book, *Mastering phpMyAdmin for Effective MySQL Management*, in April 2004, and subsequently continued to specialize in publishing highly focused books on specific technologies and solutions.

Our books and publications share the experiences of your fellow IT professionals in adapting and customizing today's systems, applications, and frameworks. Our solution-based books give you the knowledge and power to customize the software and technologies you're using to get the job done. Packt books are more specific and less general than the IT books you have seen in the past. Our unique business model allows us to bring you more focused information, giving you more of what you need to know, and less of what you don't.

Packt is a modern yet unique publishing company that focuses on producing quality, cutting-edge books for communities of developers, administrators, and newbies alike. For more information, please visit our website at www.packtpub.com.

## About Packt Open Source

In 2010, Packt launched two new brands, Packt Open Source and Packt Enterprise, in order to continue its focus on specialization. This book is part of the Packt Open Source brand, home to books published on software built around open source licenses, and offering information to anybody from advanced developers to budding web designers. The Open Source brand also runs Packt's Open Source Royalty Scheme, by which Packt gives a royalty to each open source project about whose software a book is sold.

## Writing for Packt

We welcome all inquiries from people who are interested in authoring. Book proposals should be sent to author@packtpub.com. If your book idea is still at an early stage and you would like to discuss it first before writing a formal book proposal, then please contact us; one of our commissioning editors will get in touch with you.

We're not just looking for published authors; if you have strong technical skills but no writing experience, our experienced editors can help you develop a writing career, or simply get some additional reward for your expertise.

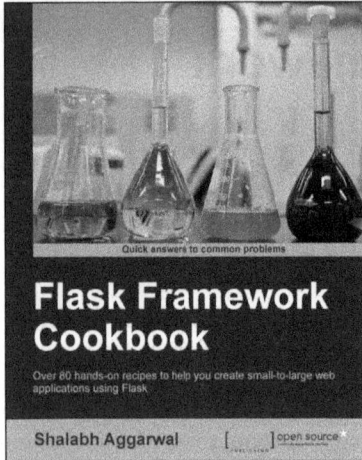

## Flask Framework Cookbook

ISBN: 978-1-78398-340-7          Paperback: 258 pages

Over 80 hands-on recipes to help you create small-to-large web applications using Flask

1. Get the most out of the powerful Flask framework while remaining flexible with your design choices.

2. Build end-to-end web applications, right from their installation to the post-deployment stages.

3. Packed with recipes containing lots of sample applications to help you understand the intricacies of the code.

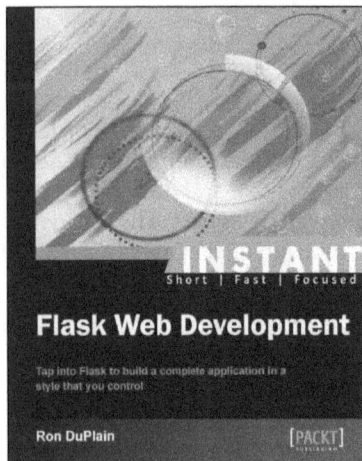

## Instant Flask Web Development

ISBN: 978-1-78216-962-8          Paperback: 78 pages

Tap into Flask to build a complete application in a style that you control

1. Learn something new in an Instant! A short, fast, focused guide delivering immediate results.

2. Build a small but complete web application with Python and Flask.

3. Explore the basics of web page layout using Twitter Bootstrap and jQuery.

4. Get to know how to validate data entry using HTML forms and WTForms.

Please check **www.PacktPub.com** for information on our titles

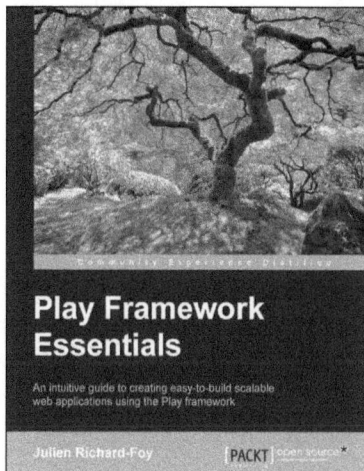

## Play Framework Essentials

ISBN: 978-1-78398-240-0            Paperback: 200 pages

An intuitive guide to creating easy-to-build scalable web applications using the Play framework

1. Master the complexity of designing a modern and scalable Web application by leveraging the Play framework stack.

2. The key concepts of the framework are illustrated with both Scala and Java code examples.

3. A step-by-step guide with code examples based on a sample application built from the ground up, providing the practical skills required to develop Scala- or Java-based applications.

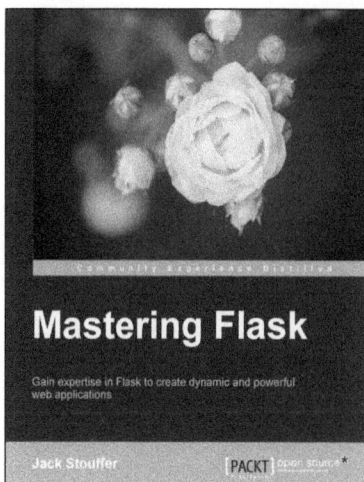

## Mastering Flask

ISBN: 978-1-78439-365-6            Paperback: 288 pages

Gain expertise in Flask to create dynamic and powerful web applications

1. Work with scalable Flask application structures to create complex web apps.

2. Discover the most powerful Flask extensions and learn how to create one.

3. Deploy your application to real-world platforms using this step-by-step guide.

Please check **www.PacktPub.com** for information on our titles

* 9 7 8 1 7 8 3 9 8 3 3 6 0 *